GLOBETR

TRAVEL G

TURKEY

JOHN MANDEVILLE

NEW
HOLLAND

GLOBETROTTER
TRAVEL GUIDE

First edition published in 1997
by New Holland (Publishers) Ltd
London • Cape Town • Sydney • Singapore

24 Nutford Place
London W1H 6DQ
United Kingdom

80 McKenzie Street
Cape Town 8001
South Africa

3/2 Aquatic Drive
Frenchs Forest, NSW 2086
Australia

10 9 8 7 6 5 4 3 2

ISBN 1 85368 635 2

Managing Editor: Clive During
Commissioning Editor: Tim Jollands
Editors: Claudia Dos Santos, Beverley Jollands
Picture Researcher: Jan Croot
Design and DTP: Sonya Cupido
Cartographers: William Smuts, Eloise Moss
Compiler: Elaine Fick

Reproduction by cmyk prepress, Cape Town
Printed in Hong Kong / China by South China
Printing Company (1988) Limited

Photographic Credits:
Abbie Enock, pages 19, 21, 69; **Chris Fairclough
Colour Library**, pages 26, 39, 60; **LF/Dr R Cannon**,
page 75; **LF/Juliet Highet**, page 57; **LF/Richard
Powers**, pages 43, 90; **LF/Flora Torrance**, pages 74,
84; **LF/Terence Waeland**, page 30; **LF/Andrew
Ward**, pages 35, 37, 38, 83; **Photobank/Adrian
Baker**, pages 78, 86; **Photobank/Jeanetta Baker**,
title page, 72, 81; **Photobank/Peter Baker**, pages 4,
12, 20, 22, 44, 73, 80; **Picture Bank Photo Library**,
page 87; **RHPL**, cover (top right), cover (bottom
right), 18, 29, 68; **RHPL/C Bowman**, page 114;
RHPL/Robert Frerck, pages 13, 23, 24, 40, 42,
62, 65, 95, 98, 119; **RHPL/Lee Frost**, page 8;
RHPL/James Green, page 14; **RHPL/Norma
Joseph** F R G S, page 6; **RHPL/Tim Megarr**,
page 55; **RHPL/Michael Short**, pages 9, 27, 45,
104, 105; **RHPL/E Simancor**, cover (top left);
RHPL/Adam Woolfitt, cover (bottom left),
pages 7, 11, 25, 28, 48, 51, 56, 66, 82, 93, 100, 106,
110, 113, 115, 116, 117; **Peter Ryan**, pages 15, 16,
17, 33, 50, 52, 54, 64, 71, 85, 97, 103, 108, 118;
Travel Ink/Ian Booth, page 10; **Travel Ink/
Dogan Kemanci**, page 36.
[LF: Life File; RHPL: Robert Harding Picture Library]

Cover Photographs:
Top left: *The outstanding ancient ruins of
the Library of Celsus at Ephesus.*
Top right: *Aya Sofya in Istanbul, once
the chief church of the Byzantine Empire.*
Bottom left: *A traditional Turkish procession,
dating from the days of the Ottoman Empire.*
Bottom right: *Ölüdeniz on the Turquoise Coast,
with its lagoon and spectacular beach.*
Title page: *The dazzling white thermal springs
of Pamukkale, formed by years of salt deposits.*

CONTENTS

1
Introducing Turkey

Turkey straddles both Asia and Europe, embracing East and West, antiquity and modern progress. This was the birthplace of the Greek civilization, a country which once ruled an empire as far-flung as that of Ancient Rome. Here you'll find all the mysterious exoticism of the East, as well as **historical sights** to match Europe's best. Visit trendy **resorts**, natural and man-made wonders, and experience a culture both familiar and enigmatic.

Istanbul has a history stretching back over two millennia and a romantic setting second to none. The spectacular domes and minarets of the grand **mosques** dominate the skyline of the **Golden Horn**, while the **Topkapı Palace** guards the exquisite treasures of the Ottoman Empire.

Along the Aegean and Mediterranean coasts you can admire some of the finest classical ruins, including entire cities such as **Ephesus** and **Pergamum**. This coastline also offers stunning **beaches**, lapped by crystal clear water, and complemented by superb scenery. The barren heartland of Anatolia contains sites dating back to the mysterious Hittite era of the Bronze Age, and the vast, incredible undergound cities and cave dwellings of **Cappadocia**. On the Black Sea coast, where Jason and the Argonauts sought the Golden Fleece, lies the legendary **Trabzon** (Trebizond), while eastern Turkey beckons with Lake Van and biblical sites such as **Mount Ararat**.

Turkey boasts one of the world's finest cuisines, as well as everything from oriental carpets and jewellery in the crowded **bazaars** to modern nightclubs in the resorts, all the products of a proud and diverse people.

TOP ATTRACTIONS

*** **Topkapı Palace:** from here the sultans ruled.
*** **Cappadocia:** cave dwellings and underground cities.
*** **Blue Mosque:** Istanbul's most famous mosque.
*** **Ephesus:** classical ruins in the eastern Mediterranean.
** **Nemrut Dağı:** carved heads on a remote mountain.
** **Sumela Monastery:** towering mountain fortress of the Byzantine Church.
** **Pergamum:** one of the great cities of the ancient world, whose library rivalled that of Alexandria.

Opposite: *Ölüdeniz, one of the finest beaches in the Mediterranean region.*

SOME GEOGRAPHICAL FACTS AND FIGURES

Highest mountain:
Mt Ararat (Agrı Dağı),
an extinct volcano with
a permanently snow-capped
peak, which rises to about
5137m (16,853ft).
Largest lake: Lake Van,
which covers an area of
approximately 3738km²
(1443 sq miles), and
reaches a depth of
about 100m (330ft).
Longest rivers: Two of the
world's greatest rivers, the
Tigris and the Euphrates,
both rise in southeastern
Turkey. The Euphrates is
some 2815km (1750 miles)
long. But the longest river,
which remains in Turkey
throughout its entire length
of 978km (607 miles), is the
Kızılırmak, which rises in the
Anatolian hinterland and
flows into the Black Sea.
Population: Turkey has
a population of about
61 million people.

THE LAND

Turkey forms part of a mountain range which arcs from
the Balkans to Iran. As this is a comparatively recent geographical phenomenon, the **mountains** are characterized
by sharp, steep peaks, making for an abundance of the
most striking scenery. The tectonic plates in this region
are unstable, which results in numerous tremors, though
ser-ious earthquakes tend to occur only infrequently,
usually in the more remote regions.

Geographically the country divides naturally into two
distinct areas: the coastal regions along the **Black Sea**,
around the **Sea of Marmara**, and along the **Aegean** and
Mediterranean shores are largely fertile, producing crops
as varied as tobacco, the famous Izmir figs, maize, nuts
and olives; the inland Anatolian region consists mainly of
mountains and a flat central plateau. Much of this land is
arable, producing over half the country's supply of grain.

Mountains and Plateaux

The average height of the Turkish land mass is 1000m
(3300ft) in the west, rising to 2000m (6500ft) in the east.
Over 90% of Turkey is mountainous, with most of the
lower, flatter terrain along the coast.

Forest-clad mountain ranges, rising to over 3000m
(10,000ft), run along the hinterland of the Black Sea and
Mediterranean coasts. Inland between them lies the vast
semi-arid Anatolian plateau. Much of this region is remin-

iscent of the Russian steppe
with its lack of trees: a flat
emptiness stretching to
immense horizons,
spanned by vast skies,
only occasionally dotted
with isolated settlements.
The region has several
large shallow salt lakes –
most notably **Tuz Gölü**
130km (80 miles) south of
Ankara – some of which
can extend for almost

1500km² (600 sq miles). There are also several extinct volcanoes in this region. The most spectacular of these is **Erciyes Dağı**, which is permanently snow-capped and rises to almost 4000m (13,000ft).

The highest peak in Turkey, also an extinct volcano, lies to the east straddling the border with Armenia and Iran. This is the imposing hulk of biblical **Mt Ararat**, which rises to 5137m (16,853ft), the spot where Noah's Ark is said to have made its first landfall after the Flood.

Rivers and Waterways

One of the most interesting geographical features of Turkey is the water link between the Black Sea and the Aegean. It is created by two narrow waterways formed from flooded river valleys: the **Bosphorus** and the **Dardanelles**, which link up with the landlocked **Sea of Marmara**. The level of the Black Sea is higher than that of the Aegean, and is constantly being filled by several of the world's greatest rivers (including the Danube, the Volga and the Dnieper). As a result both the Bosphorus and the Dardanelles, which average less than 2km (1 mile) wide, have strong southerly currents.

As is to be expected with such a vast landmass, its terrain has been carved by several widespread river systems, some of which have developed extensive flood plains. Most notable among the rivers are the Büyük Menderes, Kuçuk Menderes and Gediz, which all flow into the Mediterranean; the **Seyhan** which flows into the Mediterranean south of Adana; and Turkey's longest river, the **Kızılırmak**, which courses along for approximately 800km (500 miles) before it flows into the Black Sea. The fabled **Tigris** and **Euphrates** rivers, which once cradled ancient Mesopotamia, both rise in eastern Turkey,

Above: *Eastern Turkey is a land of dramatic vistas, by turns beautiful and forbidding.*
Opposite: *Among the country's many natural wonders are the Fairy Chimneys of Göreme in Cappadocia.*

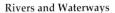

BETWEEN TWO CONTINENTS

Turkey is anchored in two continents: Europe and Asia. It has an area of 779,452km² (300,868 sq miles). Only 3% of it lies technically in Europe, but this small percentage contains most of Istanbul, the country's largest city. Turkey borders on seven countries: Greece, Bulgaria, Georgia, Armenia, Iran, Iraq, and Syria.

Above: *A secluded sandy beach on the Turquoise Coast, balm to the eye.*

DANGER: OPIUM!

For years, Turkey supplied over half the world's opium, large illegal narcotics shipments passing via various Italian and French connections to the markets of Europe and America. The thriving industry centred on the southwestern Anatolian city of *Afyon* (whose name means 'opium' in Turkish). In the early 1970s, however, the USA forced Turkey to adopt a more rigorous approach to opium control. Nowadays the cultivation of poppies is strictly supervised and for medical purposes only. A word of warning: **drug smuggling** in Turkey is taken extremely seriously. Anyone caught faces a long prison sentence.

---

before flowing into Iraq and Syria respectively. Both now support vast hydro-electric dam projects, creating huge artificial lakes.

Turkey stretches across the drainage basins of both the Indian and the Atlantic oceans, the divide running approximately north–south through the eastern part of the country. East of this, the rivers drain via the Caspian Sea and the Persian Gulf. To the west, they reach the ocean by way of the Black Sea, the Aegean and the Mediterranean.

Seas and Shores

The rugged coastal region from the Dardanelles to Rhodes offers some of the finest scenery in the Aegean and is exceptionally well suited for **sailing**. Its main city, Izmir, is an industrialized sprawl, but away from here are many lively resorts, such as **Kuşadası**, with fine beaches, lively nightlife, and many scenic attractions nearby. This coastline also contains a host of superb classical sites, such as the ancient cities of Ephesus and Pergamum. The Mediterranean coastal region is more jagged and less densely populated. Its western end is dotted with some popular and very picturesque **resorts**, plus long, perfect **beaches** such as the one at Antalya and, even more notably, beside the spectacular lagoon of **Ölüdeniz** on a stretch known as the **Turquoise Coast**. Further east, large parts of this long coastline are completely unspoilt and largely uncommercialized. The Black Sea coastal region to the north is delightfully green and often attractively backed by rugged coastal mountains. Here too, you'll find large unspoilt stretches, but parts of this region can be drab compared with the spectacular visual delights of the Aegean and Mediterranean coasts.

The coastline around the Sea of Marmara contains a few gems, but is largely disappointing. Highlights are the **Marmara Islands**, which resemble those in the Aegean, and tend to attract mainly local tourists. The northern coast is largely industrialized, and the rest unexceptional.

Climate

Turkey has five main climatic regions. **European Turkey** and the coast around the Sea of Marmara enjoy a pleasant Mediterranean climate, tempered by cooler prevailing winds from the Black Sea. Winters tend to be moderate but wet. Summers are warm but seldom oppressively hot.

The **Aegean** coastal region has long, hot summers, giving way to temperate winters with plenty of rain. Spring is often a delight, with clear, crisp days and a gradual warming of temperatures.

The **Mediterranean** coastal region is much the same, except that it's hotter. This region is officially classified as subtropical, and in summer it can become unbearably hot. The **Black Sea** coast is temperate and wet.

The Anatolian **hinterland** sees extremes of temperature: long, hot and dry summers, and freezing winters. Rainfall decreases as one moves further to the east, the region close to the Syrian border being a virtual desert. In the mountains and to the east, temperatures also tend to extremes of hot and cold.

> **BIRD PARADISE**
>
> **Kuşcenneti Bird Sanctuary** lies beside Lake Kuş some 16km (10 miles) south of **Bandirma**, on the southern coast of the Sea of Marmara. Its name means 'bird paradise' and, for once, this is no exaggeration. The lake is on the main **migration routes** from Europe. Literally millions of birds pass through each year (well over 200 species have been spotted). The best time to visit the sanctuary is in October.

Below: *Opium poppies bloom in the central Anatolian springtime.*

Plant Life

The coastal regions of Turkey are covered with more or less sparse, Mediterranean-style vegetation.

The Aegean coast is famous for its **figs**, but also sports extensive **olive groves**, and **vineyards** which produce a drinkable wine. Coniferous and deciduous **forests** cover some mountainsides up to a height of 2000m (6500ft). In spring, large stretches of apparently barren hillside are suddenly transformed into a mass of colour, covered by a breathtaking variety of blooms – it is impossible to exaggerate the magnificent beauty of this season.

COMPARATIVE CLIMATE CHART	ISTANBUL				ANKARA				AEGEAN COAST			
	WIN	SPR	SUM	AUT	WIN	SPR	SUM	AUT	WIN	SPR	SUM	AUT
	JAN	APR	JULY	OCT	JAN	APR	JULY	OCT	JAN	APR	JULY	OCT
MAX TEMP. °C	11	21	35	22	7	22	36	25	19	28	38	29
MIN TEMP. °C	-4	1	11	3	5	0	10	6	4	3	21	16
MAX TEMP. °F	52	70	96	72	45	72	97	78	67	82	101	85
MIN TEMP. °F	25	34	52	38	22	32	50	43	39	38	70	62
HOURS SUN	3	6	9	6	4	8	10	5	7	10	12	7
RAINFALL in	4	2	1	3	1	1	1	1	4	2	2	2
RAINFALL mm	109	46	34	81	33	33	13	23	112	43	50	53

The barren Anatolian hinterland experiences a similar metamorphosis, with all kinds of **wild flowers**, from orchids to tulips, bursting from the seemingly arid terrain, which becomes dappled with colour.

Wildlife

The more remote regions of Turkey are still today inhabited by animals which are now virtually extinct in the rest of Europe. Wild boars, hyenas and wolves are found, as well as the occasional bear. More common though, are flocks of **mountain goats**, and occasional glimpses of gazelles, deer and buffalo.

The country is particularly rich in **bird life**. Partridge and quail are native, but the country also plays host to a large variety of migratory birds. Turkey is on the main migration routes from Europe to Africa via the Middle East, and birds of passage include swallows, storks, and a wide range of geese.

The Black Sea coast is renowned for its **tuna**, which circle this sea in shoals, thus providing intermittent but plentiful catches for the local fishermen. The southern and western coasts sustain a very wide variety of Mediterranean fish, as well as eels, octopus and squid, while some rivers are stocked with **trout** and **carp**. Unfortunately the number of dolphins is rapidly decreasing.

Many species of **snake** inhabit the mountainous hinterland (though you're more likely to spot one in the talons of a buzzard high in the sky, rather than underfoot). The snakes become increasingly venomous as one ventures further into the hot, arid eastern regions, which also support scorpions.

Mosquitoes and many other flying **insects** inhabit the flat flood plains, though the spraying of insecticide has reduced this menace around the more popular tourist spots.

Below: *A young mountain goat, a common sight in the Anatolian highlands.*

HISTORY IN BRIEF

Archaeological evidence suggests that Anatolia has been inhabited since at least 7000BC. The earliest **Stone Age** community ever discovered was found at **Çatal Höyük**, near Konya, where the *tumuli* (earth mounds, often containing prehistoric tombs) are still visible. No less than 13 levels have been excavated here. Among the many intriguing finds are the chubby, small fertility goddesses which can now be seen in the Ankara Museum of Anatolian Civilizations.

Above: *Temple ruins at Boğazkale, once the great city of Hattuşaş.*

The Hittite Empire

At around 2000BC the people we now know as the **Hittites** arrived, almost certainly from the other side of the Caucasus. They established the first great empire in Anatolia, with their capital at **Hattuşaş** (now Boğazkale). Fascinating remnants of this once great city can still be seen scattered over a wide area.

By the 15th century BC, the Hittites had conquered **Babylon** and had even begun to rival mighty **Egypt**. The inevitable happened, and these two great empires clashed in 1275BC. The victorious Egyptians recorded the battle on the walls of the Temple of Amun at Karnak in Egypt.

Ionia

The Hittite Empire declined in the 13th century BC. This coincides with the arrival in Anatolia of a mysterious race known as the Sea People, who probably came from islands in the Aegean and may have been of Phoenician descent. By this time several kingdoms had grown up along the Anatolian shores of the Aegean. One of these was **Troy**, and it's now thought that the Trojan War (1250BC) had little to do with Helen's abduction. It is far more likely that this was a war for control of the trade route through the nearby Dardanelles to the Black Sea.

THE GORDIAN KNOT

The small town of Gordion, some 100km (65 miles) south-west of Ankara, was originally the capital of Phrygia, an early Greek kingdom. The town was named after its greatest king, Gordios. According to legend, a lowly peasant named Midas fulfilled an oracle's prediction, that the first man to enter the city gates would become its new king, since **King Gordios** had no heirs. In gratitude, Midas pledged a chariot to the deities, tying shaft and yoke with a mighty knot. It was said that whoever succeeded in untying it would become ruler of Asia. **Alexander the Great** arrived here in 334BC on his campaign of conquest, and it was he who solved the problem, by simply slicing the knot in two with his sword. Whether or not this was the intended solution, Alexander certainly went on to fulfil the predicted destiny.

Above: *Ancient greats such as Thales and Hippodamus once walked through the gateway of the theatre at Miletus.*
Opposite: *Arycanda's ancient theatre dates back to the 5th century BC.*

After the fall of Troy, **Greek colonies** began to spread all along the Aegean and Mediterranean coasts of Anatolia, founding colonies like Lydia, Lycia, Pamphylia and Cilicia.

The Aegean coastal region of Anatolia became known as Ionia, and is today generally recognized as the cradle of the Greek civilization. Cities in this region grew rich, establishing maritime trade links as far afield as Egypt and the south of France. In the 6th century BC the city of Miletus produced Thales, who is regarded as the first philosopher. Another citizen of Miletus, the architect Hippodamus, introduced the first grid plan, after a war with the Persians had virtually annihilated the city. The foundations for Western civilization were being laid. Within two centuries, many new forms of knowledge – such as geometry, physics, and biology – came into being. Today the ruins of Miletus are obscure. The coastline has shifted and buried the remains, leaving only the theatre, ruined baths and market places, surrounded by the marshlands of the Büyük Menderes flood plain.

Other Ionian cities and their rulers retain legendary status. **King Midas** was renowned for his wealth, according to myth all he touched turned to gold. Richer still was **King Croesus** of Lydia, whose capital was at Sardis (modern Sardes). Croesus and his subjects possessed so much gold that they needed a handy method for distributing it – and invented coinage. King Mausolus of **Halicarnassos** (today's Bodrum), was more concerned with the next life, and built himself a huge tomb which became one of the Seven Wonders of the Ancient World.

From the middle of the 6th century BC, the fragile network of Ionian city states faced a new threat. The huge Persian army overran Anatolia, but never managed to conquer Greece, where the civilization, which had grown up in Ionia, continued to flourish and develop.

THE COMING OF ISLAM

The prophet Mohammed was born in Mecca around AD570. The religion he founded was to galvanize the Arabs, and in the 7th century they invaded Anatolia, even reaching the shores of the Bosphorus. But they soon withdrew, consolidating their conquests throughout the Middle East and North Africa. As the Arabs departed from Anatolia, they made contact with a Turkoman tribe called the Şelcuks, who adopted the Muslim religion. These were the first true Turks to establish themselves in Anatolia.

Two centuries later Anatolia was conquered by a Macedonian Greek army under the command of **Alexander the Great**. When, in 323BC, Alexander died unexpectedly, Anatolia fragmented into a number of separate states as his generals struggled for power.

The Roman Era

At the end of the 2nd century BC the Roman Empire gradually expanded into Anatolia. By 133BC they had occupied the Aegean coast; within a century, the entire Anatolian peninsula had been incorporated. They named this new territory **Asia Minor**. (Asia, or Asia Major, referred only to the Ionian region and the immediate hinterland.)

But Asia Minor proved a troublesome spot and was shaken by several rebellions. In 74BC Mithradates Eupator, notorious King of Pontus, the kingdom bordering the Black Sea, rose and slaughtered a large proportion of the Romans who had settled along the Ionian coast. Not until **Julius Caesar** arrived on the scene did he meet his match. Julius Caesar was back a quarter of a century later as emperor, to put down another rebellion in the Pontus. This time his army crushed Mithradates Eupator's son. It was during this campaign that he coined his famous motto: '*Veni, vidi, vici*' (I came, I saw, I conquered).

During the 1st century AD, **Christianity** began to spread through the coastal cities of south and west Anatolia. St Luke is thought to have brought the aged **Virgin Mary** to live in Ephesus, and **St Paul** established several early Christian communities along the Anatolian shoreline, preaching as far inland as Galatia (Ankara).

Three centuries later the emperor himself was a Christian, but the empire had begun to crumble and Emperor Constantine moved its capital east, from Rome to Byzantium (modern Istanbul).

BARBAROSSA

The pirate-admiral who ruled the Mediterranean for the Ottoman Empire, Barbarossa ('red beard'), was born towards the end of the 15th century on the Aegean island of Lesbos. His original name was Khayr al-Din and his mother was almost certainly Greek. He and his older brother, Arouj, established themselves as pirates, terrorizing the Barbary Coast (North Africa). They were so successful that they attempted to set up a kingdom here for themselves. When the Spanish attacked, Barbarossa sought help from the Turks and as a result Algeria and Tunisia became part of the Ottoman Empire. As reward for this acquisition, Barbarossa was made high admiral of the Turkish fleet and ruled the Mediterranean, devoting his life to ferocious attacks on Christian ships and coastal towns, striking fear wherever his vessels appeared.

THE FRAGMENTATION OF THE BALKANS

The decline of the Ottoman Empire led to a volatile political situation in the Balkans. By the early years of the 20th century a number of small, independent, but fundamentally unstable states had emerged. Serbia, Albania, and Montenegro soon became embroiled in wars with their Balkan neighbours, often with three sides emerging. This situation contributed directly to World War I. Now, some three-quarters of a century later, the Balkans are in an uncannily similar situation, with countries like Serbia and Montenegro clamouring for sovereignty. The Muslims of this region are ethnic slaves who converted to Islam under Turkish rule during the period of the Ottoman Empire. To this day, racist military officers of both the Croats and the Serbs are in the habit of referring to them as 'Turks'.

Byzantium

While Byzantium was renamed Constantinople after its founder, the surrounding domain came to be known as the Byzantine Empire. When, during the 5th century, Rome was overrun by the Visigoths, the Byzantine Empire was all that remained of former glory days, as Europe descended into the Dark Ages.

The middle of the following century constituted a high point in the Byzantine Empire. The **Emperor Justinian** built the magnificent **Aya Sofya** in Constantinople, which was to remain the greatest church the world had ever seen for almost 1000 years.

This empire was to suffer many vicissitudes, however, with threats coming from both east and west. Its most serious setback occurred at the hands of the **Crusaders**, who sacked Constantinople in 1204.

Meanwhile a new people had started to venture into eastern Anatolia. These were the **Selçuk Turks**, a Tartar tribe of Turkoman origin from central Asia, who had adopted the Muslim religion. They were the forerunners of the **Ottomans**, who eventually overran all of Anatolia, taking Constantinople in 1453 under Sultan Mehmet II (the Conqueror), who banned the customary looting and destruction of its buildings and renamed the city **Istanbul**.

The Ottoman Empire

By the time **Suleiman the Magnificent** became sultan in the 16th century, the powerful Ottoman Empire covered most of North Africa and stretched as far west into Europe as the gates of Vienna, while extending east as far as the Yemen and the Persian Gulf. The Turkish fleet, under Barbarossa, ruled the Mediterranean.

On the whole, this was no vicious crushing empire. Ottoman rule was pleasantly easy-going in most instances and subjects were left to go about their business apart from the collection of taxes and occasional recruitment into the Turkish army. Members of the so-called **Janissary Corps**, the scourge of Europe, were initially forcibly recruited exclusively from among the sons of the Christian population of captured provinces. Recruits were converted to Islam, and originally celibacy was enforced – a sure-fire method of inducing ferocity.

Despite its generally lax attitude the Ottoman Empire brooked no internal rebellion, and local uprisings were quelled ruthlessly by the Janissaries.

Yet by the end of the 17th century the Ottoman Empire had begun an inexorable decline and the court of the sultan became notorious for its nasty intrigues and incompetent rule. Instead of the capable early sultans, such as Selim the Grim, there succeeded the degenerate likes of Ibrahim the Mad. The collapse of the Ottoman state was a long and complex one.

By the 19th century, Turkey was regarded as **'the Sick Man of Europe'**, and attracted the attentions of expansionist European powers (Russians, Austro–Hungarians, British, French and Germans). In the early 19th century, several of its captive nations, among them the Greeks, Bulgarians and Egyptians, had managed to achieve their independence, and in the 1850s the Crimean War erupted, partially due to Russian expansionist aims. The Turkish loss of the **Balkans** led to the chaotic Balkan Wars (1912–13) – a prelude to World War I.

World War I

Turkey entered World War I on the side of the German–Austro–Hungarian forces, in an effort to regain its lost territories. In 1915 the British and the French mounted an invasion on the **Gelibolu** (Gallipoli peninsula), which was brilliantly resisted by **Mustafa Kemal**, but defeat at the end of World War I brought ruin and widespread disillusionment. Turkey was divided into allied 'spheres

Above: *Sultan Mehmet II, conqueror of Byzantium.*
Opposite: *The Aya Sofya, an architectural wonder built in the 6th century.*

EMPEROR CONSTANTINE

Constantine was born in the Balkans around AD280 and grew up at the court of the Emperor Diocletian. During the civil wars that racked the Roman Empire at that time, he led several armies, eventually taking over as emperor. Originally a worshipper of the sun, he later attributed his success to Christianity, having been spectacularly converted when he saw a shining cross in the sky. Although deeply religious, his theology was shaky, and as a result his Christianity retained certain elements of sun-worship. His first monuments and the coins of his new eastern capital bore solar symbols as well as the Christian cross.

HISTORICAL CALENDAR

c7000BC Human settlements at Çatal Höyük.
2000 Hittites arrive in central Anatolia.
1300 Collapse of Hittite Empire.
1250 Trojan War; Greek colonization.
550 Persian King Cyrus invades Anatolia.
334 Alexander the Great conquers Anatolia.
250 Great era of Pergamum.
130 Anatolia becomes a Roman province.
c50 St Paul preaches Christianity in Mediterranean and Aegean cities of Anatolia.
AD324 Emperor Constantine moves capital of the Roman Empire from Rome to Byzantium.
c550 Emperor Justinian constructs Aya Sofya.
c1050 Invasion of Selçuk Turks from Persia.
1204 Constantinople sacked by Crusaders.
1453 Constantinople falls to Sultan Mehmet the Conqueror. End of Byzantine Empire.
c1540 Height of Ottoman Empire.

1683 Turkish siege of Vienna.
1830 Greece independent of Ottoman rule.
1912 Start of Balkan War.
1914 World War I, Turkey joins German and Austro–Hungarian allies.
1915 Gallipoli Campaign.
1919 Mustafa Kemal (later Atatürk) leads War of Independence.
1922 Atatürk takes control of Turkey.
1938 Atatürk dies.
1939–45 World War II, Turkey remains neutral.
1960 Military coup heralds period of instability.
1971 Second military coup.
1973 Democratic elections.
1980 Third military coup.
1983 Return to civilian rule.
1993 Tansu Çiller becomes Turkey's first female Prime Minister.

Below: *A Turkish army veteran who served under Atatürk.*

of influence', the sultanate was reduced to puppet status, and in 1920 the Greeks invaded, with the intention of annexing as much territory as possible.

Atatürk

One man saved the day. Mustafa Kemal rallied the Turkish forces, which drove out the Greeks. He took control of the country, the last sultan was deposed, and Kemal became president of the newly declared republic, taking on the name **Atatürk**. This surname, meaning Father of the Turks, was bestowed upon him by the Grand National Assembly when all Turks were required to select a family name as part of the social reform.

Atatürk quickly lived up to his name, rousing Turkey into action. An extensive modernization programme was begun, with the aim of transforming Turkey into a modern European state. Symbols of the old days, such as the *fez* (brimless felt or woollen cap worn by men and usually

Left: *After World War I, Atatürk erected a memorial to all those who lost their lives at Gallipoli.*

adorned with a black tassel) and the veil were banned, and the conservative power of the religious authorities was annulled. The capital was transferred from Istanbul, with its Ottoman imperial associations, to **Ankara**, in the middle of the Anatolian plateau, where a new city was built to house the administration.

Atatürk instituted wide-ranging **reforms**, designed to propel Turkey into the modern world. Among these was the abolition of Arabic script (and introduction of the European alphabet), reform of the education and legal systems, the abolition of polygamy, and the introduction of women's right to vote and hold public office. Atatürk's campaign was successful, but the strain of trying to drag his country forward in such an energetic manner eventually took its toll. In 1938, after ruling for just 15 years, Atatürk died of cirrhosis of the liver. Largely as a result of his diplomatic initiatives, Turkey managed to remain neutral in World War II.

Turkey since World War II

The post-war era has seen periods of consolidation and advance, marred by escalating inflation and unemployment, political unrest and high taxes. Growing Muslim fundamentalism and increasing agitation for Kurdish independence have not improved the unstable situation, and as a result, much of the southeastern region of the country remains under virtual military rule.

FROM ARABIC TO ABC

When the nomadic Turkic peoples converted to Islam in the 7th century, their language was written down in the script of the Koran, Arabic. However, the transliteration of Turkish into Arabic remained problematic. The sound of many Arabic letters simply didn't match the Turkish pronunciation, which brought about difficulties in teaching the written language. By the early decades of this century, the problem had become a serious impediment to the spread of literacy. It was dramatically and drastically solved by Atatürk in 1928, when he decided that Turkish should be transliterated into European lettering and had the Arabic version of Turkish banned.

MONEY IN HAND

In the early 1920s, the per capita income of Turkey was the equivalent of just US$35. Not until 1940 did it reach US$103. By the end of World War II this figure had almost quadrupled. After the war, the Turkish per capita income oscillated rapidly, dropping to US$194 in 1961, before rising to US$1164 by the end of the decade. Since then it has continued to grow steadily, and by the end of the 1990s it had reached over US$2000. The alarming dips in these figures represent genuine hardship, especially in urban areas. However, their impact would have been softened in the majority of rural areas, which remained self-sufficient to a considerable extent and thus largely unaffected by the economy.

GOVERNMENT AND ECONOMY
The Constitution

Turkey is a republic governed by a national assembly with 450 members, who are elected for five years. The powers of this assembly are laid out by the 1982 constitution. (Turkey has had a number of new constitutions since the **republic** was officially declared in 1924. These have often been tailored to fit the needs of the military, after it had rendered the previous constitution redundant by seizing power. The present constitution was written after a military coup in 1980.)

The **president** of the republic is appointed by parliament, serves for seven years and is not allowed to serve two consecutive terms in office. The president has extensive powers, which include the rights to dissolve the national assembly, call referendums, and to veto any constitutional amendments voted by the national assembly. The president also appoints all civil and military judges. However, most of the day to day running of the country is done by the **prime minister**, who must control a majority vote in the national assembly in order to pass legislation. Should legislature deny a vote of confidence, prime minister and cabinet are forced to withdraw from office.

Politics

The main political parties in Turkey are the Motherland Party (centrist), the True Path Party (centre-right) and the Prosperity Party (radical, with Muslim fundamentalist leanings). Each of these at present accounts for around 20% of the votes cast. Minority parties represent various leftist causes, the extreme right and the Kurds. Some representatives of the latter have recently been tried for sympathizing with outlawed Kurdish liberation movements and their terrorist supporters. To a certain extent, this has served to diminish Kurdish belief in Turkish democracy even further.

LOCAL GOVERNMENT

Turkey is divided into 67 provinces, each of which is overseen by a governor who represents the central government. Local government consists of elected councils and mayors. These usually stand as representatives of the main political parties. The local councils are empowered to raise taxes, and can apply to central government for subsidies and loans.

In the most recent elections the Prosperity Party emerged with the most votes, but owing to its fundament-alist leanings and anti-European stance it was unable to form a coalition government. Turkish politics, seldom stable at the best of times, look likely to remain a difficult issue. The current economic hardship has served to fuel fundamentalist, anti-European, and anti-American feel-ings. Democracy in Turkey is a fragile affair, bedevilled by a history of blunt military take-overs. It is unlikely that the Muslim fundamentalists will ever take over the country (or be allowed to do so by the army). However, the army is well aware of previous catastrophes resulting from its intervention. Meanwhile, the examples of Iran and Algeria remain a chilling reminder of what could happen. All parties are aware of this, and all (including the funda-mentalists) seem keen on avoiding such a conflict.

A DELICATE SUBJECT

Talk with any group of Turks at a café table, and chances are that at least one has worked abroad. His attitude towards you – a foreigner – will inevitably be coloured by how he was treated as a foreigner. This is not an auspi-cious beginning, as Turks are often looked down upon and discriminated against, away from home. Fortunately, their ingrained hospitality usually overcomes any lurking resentments, though these frequently resurface during discussions of controversial topics (such as Bosnia, the Muslim religion, racialism, the Kurdish question and femi-nism) which are best avoided.

The Judiciary

The independence of the judicial system is guaranteed by the constitution. Judges can only be dismissed by the Supreme Council of Judges, which also elects the mem-bers of the Final Appeal Court (known in Turkey as the Court of Cassation). A Constitutional Court decides whether laws passed by parliament are in accord with the constitution. This court is also empowered to try the president, any of his ministers, or other senior officers of state who contravene the constitution.

ECONOMIC FIGURES

The Turkish Gross National Product (GNP) escalated rapidly after Atatürk's 1922 takeover. By 1924 the GNP was growing at a rate of 15%. By the end of the decade this had risen to 22%. As a result of the World Slump, growth collapsed to 11% in 1932. After World War II the economy recovered, to grow at a slow but steady rate of 4–8%. More recently it has crept into double figures, but at the expense of heavy inflation, which has seen devaluation of the Turkish lira.

Turkey and the European Union

The Turkish government is at present faced with an almost impossible dilemma. Turkey has for some time been seeking admission to the European Community, and has made a great effort to present itself as a worthy candidate.

Despite constant friction (especially over Aegean oil rights and the Cyprus issue), Turkey has done its level best to maintain some kind of workable relation with its European neighbour and long-term foe, Greece. This has certainly helped the Turkish case for EC membership. Unfortunately, the Turks appear unable to deliver in the one area upon which the EC remains adamant: human rights. Here Turkey's record has traditionally been poor though not as bad as that of other countries at similar stages of economic development throughout the world. However, the increasing threat from the Kurdish independence movement and Muslim fundamentalism has forced the government to take a number of harsh undemocratic measures, including virtual military rule throughout western Turkey and severe action against the Kurds. Here the Turkish government has had little choice, as the alternative could well result in Turkey losing part of its eastern territory and the subsequent formation of an autonomous Kurdish state, which would destabilize the entire Middle Eastern region. Similarly, if Muslim fundamentalism became a driving force, Turkey would have no chance whatsoever of joining the EC.

Below: *Watermelons for sale, a familiar sight on city streets in summer.*

Agriculture

Turkey remains a largely rural economy, despite the increasing industrialization which has taken place over the past 40 years.

The major agricultural crops include grapes, figs, citrus fruits, tobacco and cereals. There is also widespread forestry. The farmland

Above: *On the bank of the Golden Horn, Istanbul traders sell fresh fish.*

along the coastal regions produces cotton as fibre for the clothing industry and for the extraction of oil. The fringes of this region, and the Anatolian plateau, support extensive herds of goats and sheep, and wool and leather goods are now among the country's principal exports.

Industry

To date, Anatolia has yielded few natural resources, which include a certain amount of low-grade coal and some oil. Turkey is one of the world's largest producers of chromite and has a growing petroleum-refining industry. Iron ore and copper are mined and at Eskişehir, **meerschaum** (a soft white stone) is carved into the renowned Meerschaum pipes, as well as other products. But there are almost certainly largish mineral deposits, which have yet to be exploited. This underdevelopment is largely due to a lack of foreign investment, which in turn has been discouraged by the country's continuing political uncertainty and instability.

Despite ongoing industrialization efforts, Turkey continues to lag behind in competition for world markets. In the past decades the tiger economies of eastern Asia and the Pacific rim have not only overtaken Turkey, but have left it trailing. Even so, Turkey continues to hold its own in the world markets of the textile industry. Domestic appliances and the motor industry remain strong, but mainly for home consumption.

THE NESTORIANS OF MARDIN

In the remote province of Mardin in southeastern Turkey, close to the Syrian border, lives a surviving group of Nestorians. This Christian sect was founded by **Nestorius**, bishop of Constantinople in the early 5th century, who taught that Christ was two entities (one divine, one human) who co-existed but were separate. This belief was declared heretical at the Ecumenical Council of Ephesus in 431, but the sect persisted. Its followers travelled as far afield as China, where it was almost adopted as the official religion at one point. Other remaining Nestorian communities can be found in Iraq, Iran and Syria.

Above: *Turkey's varied coastline provides a perfect playground for a booming tourism sector.*

Tourism

Tourism began to take off in a big way in the early 1980s. Within a decade Turkey had become one of the major players in the Mediterranean region. Growth in tourism was particularly accelerated by the demise of Yugoslavia, and more recently by the collapse of the Turkish lira. This sector of the economy now earns the country over US$4 billion annually.

The Future

Economic and manufacturing resources indicate that Turkey is a boom waiting to happen. But will this sleeping giant just continue to doze? The next decades will probably provide a definitive answer to this question. Turkey is at present in an exceptional position. The collapse of the Soviet Union has seen the creation of nearly a dozen new central Asian republics, many of which have large Turkoman populations and naturally look to Turkey as their regional leader and role model. Some of these countries possess oil, gas and rich mineral deposits but as yet poorly developed means of exploiting this wealth. Imaginative Turkish leadership could revitalize the entire region.

Despite the fact that politicians recently played on anti-European feeling among the electorate, it seems that resistance to Turkey's closer ties with Europe remain largely rhetorical. Turkey is now part of the European Customs Union (an initial stage on the way to full EU membership), but at present, further progress is hampered by its poor human rights record. To counterbalance this, attempts are being made to forge closer links to the east, particularly with Iran, links which remain controversial and tentative.

THE TURKOMAN PEOPLE

Groups of the original Turkoman people from whom the Turks are descended, still exist throughout the Middle East (especially Iran, Syria and Afghanistan). However, by far the largest concentration (2.7 million) is to be found in the Central Asian Republic of Turkmenistan, which lies on the eastern shore of the Caspian Sea, and came into being in 1991 after the collapse of the former Soviet Union.

THE PEOPLE

The Turks include a rich **ethnic mix**. Over the past millennia, countless invaders left their racial mark on the nation. These mainly included the **Greeks**, **Armenians** and **Mongols**, all of which have now, more or less, been absorbed into the Turkoman majority. The **Turkoman** people began arriving in Anatolia from central Asia in the 11th century, and within 400 years had completely occupied the country.

Further ethnic mixing took place during the rule of the Ottoman Empire, when several Turkic groups living in the Caucasus and around the Black Sea migrated into Anatolia.

The result of all this is that the Turkish people include a wide range of racial types. Although dark-haired Turkic–Mediterranean types predominate, it is not unusual to see several blond, blue-eyed Turks, Turks with hooded, Asiatic eyes, and Turks with a distinctly Arabic appearance. Skin colours range from fair to sallow (the predominant colouring) and dark. There are even red-haired Turks with freckles, a legacy of the invasion of the **Galatians**, who are thought to have been of Celtic origin.

Despite all this racial intermingling, there remain two distinct minority groups: the Kurds, and to a lesser extent the Arabs. The Kurds account for around 20% of the population, with their main concentration in the remote eastern section of the country. True **Arabs** are found almost exclusively in the southeast of the country, and make up less than 1% of the population. The main cities still have small communities of Turkish Jews, Greeks and Armenians.

YILMAZ GÜNEY

One of Turkey's foremost film makers was Yılmaz Güney who died in 1984. Unfortunately you won't be able to see his films in Turkey, because they are all banned for political reasons. Güney was a leftist and his work contained many harsh criticisms of the regime. His masterpieces *Yol* (The Road) and *Duvar* (The Wall) crop up every now and again at art cinemas in Europe and America. They're in no way 'difficult' and offer a genuine and sympathetic insight into modern Turkish society.

Below: *Traditional water pipes are a common feature of Turkish café society.*

Daily Life

In practice, Turkey is a class-layered society like any other. The two most decisive factors are much the same as those elsewhere – money and education. An additional element, often dependent upon the latter, is the degree of modern outlook (which in practice denotes the level of Westernization). Inevitably, urban dwellers tend to adopt a more modern approach, but increasing emigration to (and return from) Europe has also had its influence in the countryside, visible in Western clothing, as well as more hard-headed commercial attitudes and ambitions.

Despite this, life in the villages and small towns of provincial Anatolia goes on much as before. Men do men's work, the women do the rest. This means that women have almost all the work, while the men 'supervise' (often from the café). As a result, women have largely taken over the running of the home, where stricter rules tend to apply. **Segregation** of the sexes remains strongly established, and men and women (even if married) will not display affection towards one another in the presence of others. Naturally, such restraints are breaking down among the urbane youth, but this trend is counterbalanced by the rise in fundamentalist views. The black beard for young men and the *chador* (a plain head scarf worn by modern Muslim women) are no rarity in the student quarters of Istanbul these days.

The mainstay of Turkish society is the family. Marriage is a big event, celebrations often lasting for days on end. Arranged marriages are not uncommon, and the dowry system is widespread. In the villages a married son will often continue to live in his father's house with his bride, until alternative accommodation becomes available. The average size of a Turkish household is between five and six (not including young children). Families are close-knit, and kinship ties strong. The father is very much the head of the household, and is shown due respect.

Left: *A schoolchild lays a wreath of flowers at Atatürk's tomb.*
Opposite: *Provincial life: women washing carpets in the river below the citadel at Kars.*

Education

Only about 10% of the Turkish population was literate at the formation of the Turkish Republic in 1922. The same approximate figure nowadays accounts for the illiteracy rate, a remarkable achievement set in motion by Atatürk. Today, the emphasis remains secular and technological. State education is free at all levels. There are almost a dozen state-run universities or university colleges, as well as two US-funded private universities, where classes are conducted in English.

Work

As with all developed and developing countries, unemployment has become a social scourge. Exact figures are difficult to ascertain. Minimal agricultural production, **seasonal** work, and thus forced emigration, help to conceal the truth – which, according to some experts, would reveal that at least one in five of the workforce is under- or unemployed.

It's estimated that nearly two million Turks are at present '**guest workers**' in Germany, while almost a quarter of a million work in both Holland and France.

The recent slump in the European economy has forced migrant Turks to search for work elsewhere, with the majority now travelling to the Gulf and Libya. Once again, realistic figures are difficult to come by, largely owing to illegal migration.

THE TURKISH LANGUAGE

A number of Turkish words are phonetic renderings of their European equivalent. Here are a few examples you are likely to come across:

Büfe ● Buffet
Beysbol ●
A popular American game
Şarküteri ●
Charcuterie (prepared meat)
Kuafor ●
Coiffure (ladies' hairdresser)
Psikiyatrist ● For those with mental problems
Feribot ● Ferry
Milyon ● 1,000,000

Above: *Though laid on specially for visitors, performances at Ephesus give a flavour of traditional Turkish folk dance.*

Religion

During the Ottoman era, **Muslim** religion and state affairs were closely identified. In 1923 Atatürk decreed a new **secular state**. However, despite this separation of religion and state, 99% of modern Turks are Muslims. The majority of Turkish Muslims are orthodox **Sunnis**, with the remainder being **Shi'ite**. Most Turks take a fairly moderate attitude toward their religion. Alcohol, shunned by the more devout Muslims, is widely available and the majority of Turks no longer publicly observe the five daily calls to prayer. Despite this generally relaxed attitude, most Turks remain reverent, and any comment (untoward or otherwise) against the Muslim faith is liable to cause extreme offence.

Festivals

The main festivals of the Turkish year follow the Muslim calendar. **Ramadan** is marked by 40 days of fasting, food only being eaten during the hours between sunset and sunrise. Ramadan is followed by **Şeker Bayrami** (the Sugar Festival), when families and relatives exchange sweets. **Kurban Bayrami**, the Feast of Sacrifice, echoing Abraham's sacrifice of his son, follows 68 days after the end of Ramadan. Families buy a live sheep or lamb, which is then slaughtered (often in the street) accompanied by prayers and singing, after which the meat is usually distributed to the poor. A word of warning: try to avoid travelling during these times as most modes of transport are jam-packed (and often fully booked out).

Cultural Life

Turkey's rich cultural tradition has absorbed influences from many sources. The first Turkoman people were little more than **nomadic** tribesmen, with a primitive way of life and a loose animist religion. By the 11th

---

CLASSICAL MUSIC

Turkish classical music dates from the Ottoman era, and has developed a distinctive and subtle style of its own. The best place to listen is at one of the Sunday morning concerts given in Istanbul by *Klâsik Icra Heyeti*.

century they had taken on the Muslim religion, and absorbed the first elements of Persian and Arabic culture. The remnant Byzantine civilization added a new inspiration, particularly in architecture. But the Ottoman Turks quickly transcended this, developing a superb architecture of their own, which reached its peak in the construction of the great mosques. When the Ottoman Empire expanded into eastern Europe, it absorbed certain European traits. Then, with the collapse of the sultanate in the early years of the 20th century, modern European influences prevailed. The transformation of Turkish by means of a European alphabet played a major part in encouraging writers to look to Europe for modernistic inspiration, rather than to the more arcane culture of the Middle East.

Craftwork

Turkish carpets and **kilims** are renowned throughout the world. Prices vary according to the material the carpet is woven from, how closely it is woven, the quality of the dyes, the expertise of the craftsman, and the complexity of the design. Age and condition also play a part. A word of warning: the smuggling of antiques and ancient carpets is strictly illegal and carries heavy prison sentences.

Traditionally the finest Turkish **ceramics** came from Iznik. Many modern reproductions are exquisitely beautiful and marvellously decorated with fine colours and glazes. Likewise, the **copperware**, **leather goods**, **alabaster** and **Meerschaum pipes** are worth searching for. As with all such tourist-oriented mass productions, quality ranges from superb to plain awful. Fortunately, the better quality goods predominate, and there are usually bargains to be had, if you're willing to do a bit of friendly haggling.

FOOTBALL MANIA

The Turks are obsessed with sport, and by far the most popular is football. At weekends, and during the mid-week matches, life grinds to a virtual halt. What appears to be the entire male population of the nation watches TV – at home, in the cafés, through shop windows – anywhere. In smaller towns, even the traffic stops, and there's no hope of being served in a restaurant. It's never difficult to tell when the home team is winning, as being a spectator is not considered a passive activity in Turkey. But when the opposing team scores, the silence can be deafening.

Below: *Designs in flatweave kilims often include stylized birds and animals.*

A FAVOURITE
HORS D'OEUVRE

Among the many titbits laid out for mezes, you may notice plates of small stuffed aubergines. These will have been roasted and filled with either garlic and tomato, or sometimes spicy rice with currants and lamb. This dish is called *imam bayıldı* – which in Turkish means 'the imam fainted.' The name is said to derive from the delight displayed by a Muslim priest when he was offered this dish for the first time.

Opposite: *Traditional fare: coffee, sticky* baklava *and Turkish Delight.*
Below: *Tranquility and peace inside the domed interior of a Turkish bath.*

Sport and Recreation

No summary of Turkish cultural life would be complete without mentioning Turkey's most popular leisure activity by far: watching football on TV. The entire country appears to grind to a halt when matches are played.

Basketball and wrestling are also popular. The famous oiled wrestling championships take place each June at **Edirne** (*see* p. 51). Another indigenous sport is **camel-wrestling**, which takes place in Aydın province (near Izmir) during winter.

All the usual watersports abound at the coastal resorts. The crystal waters and rocky shoreline of the Mediterranean and Aegean coasts are ideal for snorkelling and scuba diving. Equipment can be hired, but you'll need a Certificate of Competence for diving. Marmaris is famous as a **yachting** centre, with a wide variety of craft for hire.

Another great Turkish cultural institution is the *hamam* (**Turkish bath**). Each town has its own public hamam, and no visit to Turkey would be complete without a visit to at least one of these tranquil havens.

Food and Drink

The Turkish nomads of central Asia may have had little time for the delicate niceties of the kitchen, but they bequeathed to the world three important culinary inventions. *Şiş* consists of small pieces of skewered meat which are cooked over an open fire. These **kebabs** made an ideal meal for a people on the move. Those on an even faster trot and with even less time didn't cook their meat at all. The Tartar people gave us 'steak tartare'. In those early days raw meat for this dish was tenderized by being placed under a horse's saddle and ridden on for a few days, although today it's more common to use mince. The third great Turkic invention was **yoghurt**, nowadays an essential ingredient and used in a wide variety of their dishes.

Sophistication was added to the Turkish kitchen after the fall of Constantinople in the mid-15th century, when the Ottomans added the exotic delicacies of their Byzantine cuisine. Stuffed vegetables – such as aubergines and peppers – were soon a favourite, as were various spicy rice dishes, vine leaves, and many sickly-sweet cakes. Later, as the empire spread, further refinements were incorporated from such regions as the Caucasus, Eastern Europe, and Egypt.

The most obvious manifestation of the profusion of delights offered by the Turkish kitchen is *mezes*. These *hors d'oeuvres* include dishes like *humus* (a tasty chickpea dish), stuffed vine leaves, fiery garlic yoghurt and goats' cheese pie – and they taste as exciting as they look.

Kebab salons tempt with a mouthwatering variety of kebabs (usually called *kebap* in Turkey) ranging from *Bursa kebap* (with tomato, butter and yoghurt) to *Adana kebap* (which has a distinctly Middle Eastern spiciness).

No Turkish meal would be complete without a **dessert**. Be warned though: sticky, sweet cakes such as *baklava* or *burma kadayıf* come soaked in honey.

The best way to round off your meal is with a small, strong Turkish **coffee**. Avoid drinking to the bottom of the cup, which is invariably muddy. To aid your digestion, you can then try a small glass of fiery raki, which resembles the French *pastis*. Contrary to Muslim taboo, **alcohol** is readily available in almost all urban areas and resorts. You will even find it served in remote villages. In the holy cities, however, alcohol is more restricted.

Turkey's main beer is *Efes* (Ephesus). Turkey also produces wines, most of which are quite drinkable. The local hootch, **raki**, tastes of anis and turns white when you add water to it, a wise precaution, as it does have quite a kick.

TURKISH WATER

In cities and resorts it is usually safe to drink from the tap, though the water tends to be heavily chlorinated and sometimes has a cloudy colour, leaving an unpleasant aftertaste. In country areas you are best advised not to drink tap water. Bottled mineral water is available in most stores.

TURKISH COFFEE AND TEA

Turkish coffee is served in tiny cups. It is usually quite strong and the bottom of the cup will have a muddy residue which is best left. Nowadays Turkey imports most of its coffee from Brazil, and, owing to inflation and devaluation of the Turkish lira, the price has shot up. In cafés the most popular drink at present is tea, which comes in a small glass, without milk, but with a slice of lemon.

2
Istanbul

Technically, Istanbul lies divided, its European side separated from its Asian outskirts by the **Bosphorus** channel – vital waterlink between the Black Sea and the oceans of the world. Yet, as soon as you set foot in the city, there's no mistaking that you're in the East. It's not just the profusion of magnificent mosques, or the exotic bustle of the bazaars. The music is different, so are the people, and though the writing on the shopfronts may be in the European alphabet, it certainly looks strange.

The Old City of Istanbul (*Stamboul*), from where the sultans once ruled an empire that stretched from the Gates of Vienna to the Indian Ocean, stands on a hillside overlooking water on three sides. To the north lies the inlet known as the **Golden Horn**, to the south the blue waters of the enclosed Sea of Marmara, and to the east the Bosphorus, which is now spanned by two modern suspension bridges, the Atatürk and the Galata. It also provides one of the most romantic urban settings in the world. There are few sights to match a crescent moon rising above the domes and minarets of Istanbul, its reflection melting into the dark waters below. The best place to watch the spectacular Istanbul sunsets is down by **Galata Bridge**, on the northern shore.

If you feel the need to take a break from the clamorous commotion of Istanbul, you can always take a ferry to the **Princes' Islands** (*see* p. 43), just over 10km (6 miles) to the southeast of the city in the Sea of Marmara. Here there are a number of good beaches, as well as some pleasant walks around the shore and through woodlands.

DON'T MISS

*** **Topkapı Palace:** from here the sultans ruled their empire. Home of the dazzling Spoonmaker's diamond.
*** **Aya Sofya:** for almost 1000 years the most famous church in Christendom, called the Eye of the Universe.
*** **The Blue Mosque:** one of the great mosques of Istanbul.
** **The Princes' Islands:** holiday islands in the Sea of Marmara near Istanbul.
* **The City Walls:** walls which once guarded the ancient Byzantium.

Opposite: *The domes and minarets of Istanbul capture the mystery of the East.*

CLIMATE

The temperature in Istanbul seldom rises much above 30°C (86°F), even at the height of the summer. However, the crowded and noisy streets make it seem much hotter than this. **Autumn** is milder, but it often rains. In the winter it's cold, and frequently wet. **Spring** is by far the best time to visit Istanbul.

SIGHTSEEING IN THE OLD CITY

The streets of Istanbul reflect a rather haphazard blend of ancient and modern. Car horns compete with transistor radios blaring quarter-tone oriental music. Old men, ceaselessly fingering long strings of worry beads, share a *hookah* pipe at the café, while their sons sit glued to the TV screens watching football. Strictly dressed fundamentalist young women mingle with their 'jeans generation' peers.

In high summer the combined heat and clamour of the streets can become oppressive. An element of culture shock is inevitable: but it needn't prove to be over-whelming. Take it easy to begin with. Visit the sites early in the morning, or late in the afternoon, and stop off at the cafés for a refreshing bulb glass of lemon tea.

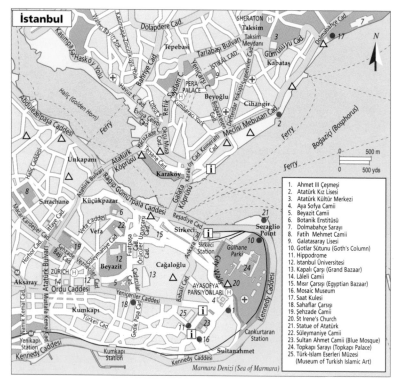

1. Ahmet III Çeşmeşi
2. Atatürk Kız Lisesi
3. Atatürk Kültür Merkezi
4. Aya Sofya Camii
5. Beyazit Camii
6. Botanik Enstitüsü
7. Dolmabahçe Sarayı
8. Fatih Mehmet Camii
9. Galatasaray Lisesi
10. Gotlar Sütunu (Goth's Column)
11. Hippodrome
12. Istanbul Üniversitesi
13. Kapalı Çarşı (Grand Bazaar)
14. Lâleli Camii
15. Mısır Çarşısı (Egyptian Bazaar)
16. Mosaic Museum
17. Saat Kulesi
18. Sahaflar Çarşışı
19. Şehzade Camii
20. St Irene's Church
21. Statue of Atatürk
22. Süleymaniye Camii
23. Sultan Ahmet Camii (Blue Mosque)
24. Topkapı Sarayı (Topkapı Palace)
25. Türk-Islam Eserleri Müzesi (Museum of Turkish Islamic Art)

Istanbul offers a host of sights, great and small, mostly in the Old City. The following attractions are listed so that you can visit them in an easy succession from east to west across the Old City.

Topkapı Palace ***

The grounds of the Topkapı Palace occupy the elevated eastern end of the Old City, the **Seraglio Point**. It's a superb site, dominating the entrance to the Golden Horn, with wonderful views across the Bosphorus towards the Asian shore.

This is the palace from which the Ottoman Empire was ruled for over 400 years, frequently by its eunuchs, harem ladies and the fearsome Janissary Corps. Surprisingly, it is not an overwhelmingly grand palace, such as Versailles or Buckingham. In fact it's an unexpectedly homely place, with shady interleading courtyards, and all its components in suitable proportion. It's easy to imagine how pleasant it could have been to live here.

The Topkapı Palace was started in the mid-15th century, just a few years after the Turks had conquered the city and made it the capital of their new empire. Over the centuries many elaborate additions were commissioned, resulting in the pleasantly unsymmetrical complex of buildings and courtyards which remains today.

You enter the main section of the palace through **Ortakapı** (the Middle Gate), which leads into the large **Second Court**. The buildings in the top lefthand corner of this courtyard are the celebrated **harem**, where visitors are allowed only on guided tours. Alas, the building is now devoid of its former inhabitants, the tour no longer conducted by a menacing, half-naked eunuch brandishing a scimitar.

> **THE ONE WHO GOT AWAY**
>
> **Sultan Ibrahim the Mad** believed in living up to his name. When he suspected one of his wives of being unfaithful to him, he flew into such a jealous rage that he ordered his entire harem to be sewn into sacks and drowned in the Bosphorus. After having been thrown overboard, only one of his wives managed to claw her way free, was rescued by a passing French ship, and managed to make her escape to France.

Below: *Baghdad Köşkü in the Topkapı Palace, long-time home to the sultans.*

**THE DESECRATION
OF AYA SOFYA**

Aya Sofya has been sacked
several times during its long
history, but the worst indig-
nity was inflicted in 1204,
when **Crusaders** captured
Byzantium and ravaged the
city. The victorious Crusaders
celebrated by getting drunk
and installing a prostitute
on the emperor's throne
in the Aya Sofya.

Contrary to popular belief, the Harem was not just
where the sultan kept his wives and concubines, it
was also the headquarters from which he ruled his entire
empire. This meant that there had to be sufficient accommodation for the various ministers, visiting generals,
advisers and the like. (Understandably, these quarters
were strictly segregated from the Harem proper, and
anyone who took the wrong turning in the maze of halls
and wings would not only encounter a fierce eunuch,
but was liable to become one himself.)

There are many other sights at Topkapı which should
not be missed. These include the fabulous decor of the
Throne Room, in the **Third Court**. This courtyard also
contains Ahmet III's superb **Library**, as well as the
Treasury, which occupies the upper righthand corner
and contains many price-less relics, including the
huge **Topkapı Diamond** (sometimes known as the
'Spoonmaker's diamond').

The Treasury also contains the enchanting
Mehmet II Pavilion, whose cool, pillared terrace
has one of the most roman-tic views of the **Bosphorus**.
Beyond is the Fourth and last Court, which looks out
over the Golden Horn. It contains the pool where
Ibrahim the Mad would cavort with his harem, as
well as the charming little pavilion known as the
Baghdad Köşkü (the latter word is the origin of our
word kiosk).

Topkapı Palace

0　　50　　100 m
0　　50　　100 yds

1　Revan Köşkü
2　Pool
3　Circumcision Room
4　Baghdad Köşkü
5　Mustafa Sofa Köşkü
6　Physician's Tower
7　Restaurant
8　Imperial Treasury
9　Museum Directorate
10　Sultans' Portraits
11　Clocks and Watches
12　Holy Relics
13　Police
14　Ahmet III Library
15　Library
16　Harem
17　Turkish Embroideries
18　Arms and Armour
19　Hall of the Divan
20　Harem Entrance
21　Imperial Stables
22　Palace Models
23　Archive
24　Doctor
25　Chinese and Japanese Porcelain
26　Silverware and Crystal
27　Kitchen
28　Ottoman Glassware and Porcelain
29　Sultans' Costumes
30　Throne Room

Marble Terrace　**Fourth Court**

Harem Garden

Terrace of the Favourite

Mehmet II Pavilion

Third Court

W.C.

Gate of Felicity

Second Court

Ortakapı (Middle Gate)　**First Court**

Ticket Booth

N

Aya Sofya ★★★

The name of this massive, domed, red church means 'divine wisdom' in Greek. It stands on **Sultanahmet Square**, just across from the Blue Mosque, in the heart of the Old City.

Aya Sofya was built in the 6th century by the Roman **Emperor Justinian**. By this time

Above: *Four minarets surround the central dome of Istanbul's Aya Sofya.*

the Empire had converted to Christianity and its capital had moved here, to what is now Istanbul. The construction of Aya Sofya was so vast and ambitious a project that it is said to have taken 10,000 men almost six years to achieve, and all but bankrupted the Roman Empire. Building material used in its construction was looted from as far afield as Ephesus (in Aegean Turkey) and Baalbek (in modern-day Lebanon).

Inside its gloomy darkness, one is immediately overwhelmed by the huge, chilly inner spaces, topped by a truly awesome **dome** and often slashed by dramatic rays of sunlight. For over a thousand years this was the largest enclosed space in the world. The enormous central dome spans over 30m (100 feet) and receives no support except from the massive buttresses at its rim, an amazing architectural feat at the time. In the northern aisle you can see the famous '**Weeping Column**'. Poke your finger into the well-worn hole of this pillar and make a wish. If your finger emerges damp, your wish will come true!

Although Aya Sofya was sacked several times during its long history, its marvellous treasures looted or destroyed, many of the fine mosaics of saints and emperors have survived to this day. After the fall of the city to the Turks in 1453, Aya Sofya became a mosque, until Atatürk had it classified as a museum in 1936. Open 09:30–16:30, Tuesday–Sunday.

Above: *The magnificent domed interior ceiling of the Blue Mosque.*
Opposite: *The Grand Bazaar consists of several different atmospheric markets or districts.*

IZNIK TILES

Nowadays, Iznik is just a small lakeside town southeast of Istanbul. During the 15th century, Mehmet I brought some 500 captured potters from Persia to Iznik, who introduced the secrets of their art into Turkey. The result was a flourishing trade in exquisitely hand-decorated tiles, many of which contained a copper blue which had hitherto been unobtainable outside Persia. At its height, over 300 kilns produced ceramics and tiles here, which were transported throughout the Ottoman Empire to decorate mosques and other buildings.

The Blue Mosque ★★★

Known by the Turks as the **Sultan Ahmet Camii**, this is the magnificent mosque across the square from Aya Sofya, which dominates the Old City skyline, overlooking the Sea of Marmara, the Golden Horn and the Bosphorus.

As you approach from the northeast you see the complex multi-domed structure rising to the central dome, overlooked by six slender **minarets**, each with three circular balconies. These few slim towers caused great consternation when they were built, for it meant that the Blue Mosque now had as many minarets as the chief mosque at Mecca, the Elharam. Rather than destroy the pleasing symmetry of the Blue Mosque, the sultan overcame this problem by having a seventh minaret built at the Elharam Mosque. The Blue Mosque's minarets make a useful landmark if you get lost in the **Sultanahmet** district.

Inside, the walls are covered with over 20,000 blue Iznik tiles, and the arches are inscribed with interlacing curlicues of Arabic script. The domes are supported by massive 'Elephant's Foot' pillars, and the high enclosed space is illuminated by stained glass windows. It is important to remember that, when entering a mosque in Turkey, you must always remove your shoes. Women should cover their heads and their arms, and not wear revealing dresses or shorts. Open 09:00–17:00 daily.

The Hippodrome ★★

This ancient Roman arena, which once seated up to 100,000 spectators, stands in the shadow of the Blue Mosque. The track which ran around its edges was over 1000m (1100yd) long, and was used for chariot races, which were immensely popular in ancient Byzantium. Important events attracted attendances as large as those at major modern football matches.

The Hippodrome was originally laid out in the 3rd century. Today, little remains of its former glory, except the columns in the centre of the track. The **Serpent Column** was originally made in the 6th century BC from the melted-down shields of the defeated Persian army. When **Mehmet II** conquered Constantinople he issued a decree forbidding his troops to plunder the city as was the custom, and instead struck off one of the serpent's heads in a symbolic act of vandalism.

The **Egyptian Obelisk** was created in the 15th century BC during the reign of Pharaoh Thutmose III. It was pillaged in the 4th century AD during the reign of Emperor Theodosius I and was broken in transit, but the hieroglyphs remain clearly visible.

The Grand Bazaar ★★★

Known in Turkish as the **Kapalı Çarşı**, it is the largest covered bazaar in the world. After Mehmet the Conqueror took Constantinople from the Christian Byzantines in 1453, he set about transforming the city into the capital of his new Islamic empire. To entice traders back into the deserted city and stimulate its stagnant economy, priority was given to the building of this bazaar, and it was completed well before the Topkapı Palace and the city's first new mosque.

Over the centuries the Grand Bazaar suffered many catastrophes. It burnt down several times, and was reduced to a huge field of rubble after an earthquake. The bazaar may at first appear to be a maze-like jumble of alleyways, but is in fact laid out on a clear grid pattern. This layout divides the bazaar into separate districts, which specialize in different goods. The central **İç Bedesten** (the Old Market) specializes in antiques, silver-

ware and copper items. South of here, along **Keseciler Caddesi**, are the bag shops. To the west of Iç Bedesten is **Takkecilar Sokak**, where you can find yet more antiques and silverware. The oldest part of the Bazaar is **Sahaflar Çarşisi**, a corner of which has been devoted to selling ancient books since Byzantine times. Other streets used to be named after the trade which was practised in them: Sword-makers' Street, Jewellers' Alley and so forth. Nowadays many of these trades have moved elsewhere.

The Bazaar can get hot and crowded, and pickpockets are not uncommon (be sure to hang on to your bag). But you're never far from a cold-drink stand or fountain. Many of the stallholders are genuinely friendly and enjoy **bargaining** with you over a cup of Turkish tea (after all, they're better at it than you are). And for your part, there are all kinds of bargains to be had – from excellent leather boots and perfumes to authentically garish gold medallions and tacky nick-nacks. Open 08:30–19:00, Monday–Saturday (April–October); 08:30–18:30 (November–March).

Süleymaniye Mosque **

This mosque is in the northwestern sector of the Old City, looking down over the Galata Bridge across the **Golden Horn**.

Below: *Süleymaniye Mosque, its dome and minarets spectacularly floodlit at night.*

Many architectural historians consider this to be the very finest mosque to be built by **Mimar Sinan**, the greatest Turkish architect. He designed it in the mid-16th century, when the Ottoman Empire was at its peak, for **Suleiman the Magnificent**. In all, over 5000 workmen of the highest calibre were employed in its construction. The superb stained glass windows were the work of Ibrahim the Drunkard. The external proportions of the mosque are equally exquisite.

Its dome and minaret stand out above the western skyline of Istanbul at sunset, when seen from the famous viewing point on the quay beside the north-eastern end of Galata Bridge. The inside of the mosque was restored in the 19th century by two Swiss architects, the Fossati brothers. They saw fit to accentuate its purity of line with various Baroque flourishes, a desecration which has reduced many architectural critics to stunned silence.

Above: *This section of the Old City wall guarded the European approaches to the city.*

The graveyard by the mosque contains Suleiman's tomb. Beside him is buried his much-feared wife **Roxelana**, who exercised an ever-increasing influence over him – finally persuading him to murder the heir to the throne, so that her own son could succeed instead. Open 09:30–17:00 daily.

At the corner of the nearby street which is named after Mimar Sinan, you can see the great architect's burial place in a tomb which he designed for himself.

The Old City Walls *

The site was originally chosen by the Greeks around 3000 years ago, because of its superbly defensible position. The earliest city stood on the high promontory now occupied by the grounds of Topkapı Palace. The only defence then installed was a short land wall crossing from the Golden Horn to the Marmara shore. As the city grew, expanding up the peninsula, the fortifications gradually moved further west. (Roman defensive walls ran by the Hippodrome.)

The massive ancient walls which still dominate the western approaches to the Old City were erected by the Emperor **Theodosius II** in the 5th century. Even today, with gaps at the gates widened to allow modern roads to pass through, these walls make a forbidding sight.

TULIPS FROM ISTANBUL

One of the most colourful events of the Istanbul year is the Tulip Festival, which takes place annually from late April until early May in the northern garden suburb of Emirgan on the western shore of the Bosphorus, halfway between the two bridges. **Sultan Ahmed III** used to hold **tulip festivals** in the Topkapı palace on moonlit nights, among a profusion of tulip-filled vases and caged canaries. Tulips originated in **Mongolia**, and came to Europe via the Ottoman Empire. Here they acquired the name *tulabend*, which means 'turban'. Our name for the flower is a corruption of this word.

Above: *The Bosphorus Bridge is visible from Ortaköy, a fishing village on the European side of the water.*

It was over 500 years before the walls gave way to an enemy. In the 13th century Crusaders sailed up the Golden Horn, ran their ships alongside, and scaled the walls with ladders. Two hundred years later, they were more decisively breached by Mehmet II.

You can still wander along the remaining ramparts, which stretch for 6km (4 miles), though you have to descend at various points. The remains of several castles lie en route. Only two towers remain standing of **Ayvan Saray**, the castle which guarded the northern end of the wall. In 1453 the last Byzantine emperor, Constantine XI, rode out from this castle to surrender Constantinople to Sultan Mehmet II, who completed the fortress at the other end of the wall a few years after the fall of Constantinople. It is called **Yedikule** (Castle of the Seven Towers), venue of the sultans' main torture chamber, part of which was gruesomely but fittingly known as 'The Well of Blood'.

Museums ★★★

Among the finest museums in Istanbul are undoubtedly those in the **Topkapı Palace**. Also not to be missed is the **Museum of Turkish Islamic Art**, housed in the 16th-century palace of Ibrahim Paşa on the northwest side of the Hippodrome, which contains a superb collection of ancient Turkish carpets and many historic exhibits illustrating how ordinary people lived in Turkey from the nomadic Mongol era to the present. Attached to the Blue Mosque is the **Museum of Kilims and Carpets**, where you can admire this supreme Turkish art at its finest. Further along Kabasakal Caddesi is the **Mosaic Museum**, which contains fascinating Byzantine exhibits underground, just as they were discovered. Most museums in Istanbul are open 09:30–17:00 daily, except Monday.

THE BOSPHORUS

Even if your time in Istanbul is limited, a ferry ride on this strip of water, which divides Europe from Asia and flows through the centre of Istanbul, is well worth it. Known by the Turks for centuries as *Boğazıçı*, this waterway has always been of great strategic importance as the only waterway linking the Black Sea to the Mediterranean. In the classical era, whoever held it controlled access to the wealthy Greek trading colonies of the Black Sea.

More recently, this was the only way the Soviet Southern Fleet, based at **Odessa**, could reach the Mediterranean. Free passage of Soviet battleships and aircraft carriers through the heart of Istanbul was guaranteed by treaty, and the Soviets brooked no interference with this right whatsover.

The twisting Bosphorus has a length of around 30km (20 miles), averages a width of 3km (2 miles) between its steep banks, and is now crossed by two massive suspension bridges. If you're catching a ferry, be sure to note its destination: *Rumeli* denotes the European shore, *Anadolu* the Asian one.

Dolmabahçe Palace *

This modern palace stands outside the Old City, on the west bank of the Bosphorus. It was built in 1853, and was used as official residence by the last sultans. It is set on a historic site – that of the harbour from which Mehmet II launched his

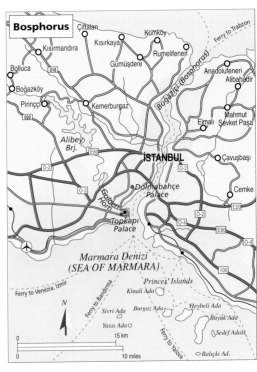

A TRAITOR'S FATE

The tower at the northern end of the Old City Walls is called **Ayvan Saray**, and was a **prison** in Byzantine times. Its most famous inmate was Michael Anemas, who had plotted to overthrow the emperor, Alexius I Comnenus, in the 12th century. As an example to any future plotters, Anemas was crowned with sheeps' entrails and led through the city streets. Then the hairs were plucked from his beard one by one. Fortunately for Anemas, the emperor's daughter took pity on him and interceded on his behalf before his eyes were plucked out.

successful attack on Constantinople in 1453. In the early 17th century **Sultan Ahmet I** had the cove filled in (an operation which required 16,000 Christian slaves) and the site was turned into a royal garden. The Turkish *Dolmabahçe* means 'filled-in garden'. Two hundred years later, **Sultan Abdul Mejid** chose this as the site for his new palace.

Compared with Topkapı, the Dolmabahçe Palace is grandiose in the crass Victorian manner. Indeed, Queen Victoria herself contributed one of its most ostentatious interior features – a colossal cut-glass chandelier weighing over 4½ tons (4500kg), which hangs from the ceiling of the **Throne Room**. Beneath this extravagant glitterball the sultans were consulted on affairs of state, while the international press was permitted to watch from behind a grille and members of the harem watched from behind another.

Visitors are conducted on an 80-minute guided tour of the palace, which includes Sultan Abdul Aziz's bed – a mammoth construction large enough to support his massive frame as well as several members of his harem. In 1923 the sultans were deposed, **Atatürk** proclaimed the Turkish Republic and was elected its first (and greatest) president. The palace now became his home, and contains the room in which he died on 10 November 1938. Open 09:00–15:00 daily, except Monday and Thursday.

Right: *The Grand Stairway of the Dolmabahçe Palace, last residence of the sultans.*
Opposite: *You can buy an elegant, traditional Turkish tea set at the Grand Bazaar.*

SHOPPING IN ISTANBUL

The best place to go shopping in Istanbul is of course the Grand Bazaar. It lures visitors with a large range of carpets and kilims, jewellery, silver and copperware, leather goods and antiques. The **bookmarket** here is noted for its antique copies of the Koran and texts containing decorative Arabic script.

Not so good for merchandise, but in a way even more picturesque, is the **Egyptian Spice Bazaar** down by Galata Bridge. Here you can pick up a fragrant variety of spices, tapes of Turkish music, as well as henna and other things.

The smarter modern section of town across the Golden Horn also has the more fashionable shops. Modern Turkish fashion accessories are available in the shops of **Rumeli Caddesi**. Nearby on **Istiklâl Caddesi** you'll find Vasko, Istanbul's main department store. But you'll probably feel a bit more at home in the **Ataköy Shopping and Tourism Centre**, the shopping mall out near the airport, where you can get everything from Benetton clothes to a Big Mac.

You'll find that you either love **Turkish music**, or loathe it. If you fall into the former category, you may wish to take home a souvenir tape. These are on sale at shops all over Istanbul. Classical Turkish music can be extremely subtle, but the music you hear blaring out all over the place is usually Turkish pop.

The City at Night **

Istanbul is very much a night-time city and restaurants and clubs hum with activity in the evening. If you wish to enjoy a night out at a club where you can see some skilful **belly dancing**, try Kervansaray Nightclub close to the Hilton at 30 Cumhuriyet Caddesi. (The prices tend to be rather Hilton too.)

For an excellent free show, try the **Sound and Light** performance which is put on at the **Blue Mosque** each evening. The best place to watch is from the benches in the gardens to the northwest of the mosque in the direction of Aya Sofya.

The famous red light district, for which Istanbul is fondly remembered by sailors throughout the world, is in the side streets off Istiklâl Caddesi. Any visitors passing through this area should take extra care to avoid being parted from their money.

For many of the locals, a night on the town often includes a visit to one of the many *gazinos*. These are old-style Turkish clubs, where singers, agile oriental dancers and jugglers entertain the customers. Drinks and *meze* are served. The younger crowd tend to opt for the entertainment of the livelier Western-style bars, such as Kedi's Bar in **Arnavutköy**.

For a truly romantic evening, try a **dinner cruise** on the Bosphorus, details of which can be found in the lobby of any luxury hotel. Some of the cruises leave from the landing stage at Eminönü.

Nightlife in Istanbul is lively, but it comes into its own when the 'glamour crew' arrives for the **Istanbul International Festival**, from the end of June to mid-July. This festival specializes in exhibitions and performances by leading Turkish performers and artists.

OTTOMAN DIPLOMACY

The machinations of the Ottoman Empire remained a mystery to Europe for many years. The rulers of France, Britain and Russia would despatch their emissaries, who, just like modern ambassadors, were expected to act as unofficial spies, reporting back to their masters about the intrigues at the sultan's court.

However, the Ottoman sultans simply refused to play this diplomatic game. As soon as an ambassador arrived to present his credentials, he would be arrested as a spy and flung into a dungeon. This practice led to a special prison being set aside, solely for use by the languishing foreign envoys. It became known as the **Tower of Inscriptions**, since the unfortunate jailbirds were in the habit of scratching their name, title and country of origin into the walls.

PRINCES' ISLANDS

These are just a two-hour ferry ride from the heart of Istanbul, and make an ideal retreat from the heat and clamour of the city. There are four main islands, each with its own particular charm.

On the largest island, **Büyük Ada**, cars are forbidden and the main means of transport is horse-drawn carriage. This is where **Trotsky** came to live in 1929, after being banished from the Soviet Union by Stalin. It is the furthest from Istanbul, and swimming on the paying beaches is not the best.

Heybeli Ada lies to the west of Büyük Ada. It has some fine scenery and beaches, which means that on summer weekends it often becomes crowded. The least crowded swimming spots are along the northern shore.

Burgaz Ada lies closer to Istanbul and is slightly smaller than the other two. This island used to be populated largely by Greeks and Jews, and you can still see the domed Greek Orthodox Church above the harbour. There is also a synagogue. One of the most fashionable beach clubs in Turkey is situated here (but you won't be able to get in unless you know a member). Inland, the hills and woods are good for walking.

Kınalı Ada is nearest to Istanbul, and surprisingly barren, but it offers some fine walks beyond the cliffs. It also has excellent views across the Sea of Marmara to the shoreline of Istanbul only 12km (8 miles) away.

DOG ISLAND

The smallest of the Princes' Islands is **Köpek Adası** – which means 'dog island'. Sadly, its name was all too apt at one stage. For years, this was where the stray dogs rounded up from the streets of Istanbul were dumped and left to fend for themselves. The sound of their pitiful howls drifting across the water eventually became too much, the necessary steps were taken and the island is now dogless.

Left: *Burgaz Ada, one of the Princes' Islands in the Sea of Marmara.*
Opposite: *The ancient art of belly dancing is an Ottoman legacy.*

Istanbul at a Glance

BEST TIMES TO VISIT

Istanbul is often oppressively hot during the summer. In autumn it's frequently dreary and wet, while the winters are usually cool. By far the best time to visit Istanbul is in **spring**. From late April to early May the city holds its Tulip Festival. Istanbul continues to enter regular bids to stage the Olympic Games which, so far, have all been unsuccessful. However, should the city succeed sometime in future, that may well be a time not to visit, as the traffic would undoubtedly be chaotic.

GETTING THERE

Istanbul's Atatürk Airport (Yeşilkoy) is 45 minutes' drive from the centre of the city. Shuttle buses to the city centre leave at regular intervals. Taxis are available at all times. These are inexpensive, but make sure you agree upon the fare to your destination before getting in.

GETTING AROUND

The best way to experience Istanbul, especially the Old City, is to walk. If you don't fancy walking or can't, taxis are plentiful and cheap. Be sure to establish the price to your destination before you get in. Tipping is not always expected, but most passengers round up their fare to the nearest 10,000 TL. The famous Turkish dolmuş (shared taxi)

system operates extensively in Istanbul. Most of these vehicles are large old-style American limousines which ply fixed routes between certain main destinations (usually marked). You hail the dolmuş, get in with the others, and get out when you want. It's cheap, but cramped. To cross the Bosphorus to the Asian shore, you can use one of the many ferries. Ferries to most destinations depart from the Bosphorus shore down by Galata Bridge.

WHERE TO STAY

LUXURY

Ayasofya Pansiyonlari, Soğukçeşme Sokak, Sultanahmet, tel: (212) 513-3660, fax: 513-3669. Superb old Turkish houses with modern conversions; along the outer walls of Topkapı Palace.

Çirağan Palace, 84 Çirağan Caddesi, tel: (212) 258-3377, fax: 259-6686. Superb Bosphorus setting. Generally reckoned to be the best in town.

Hilton Hotel, Cumhuriyet Caddesi, tel: (212) 231-4650, fax: 240-4165. One of the best of this chain. A social landmark in the city.

Sheraton Hotel, Taksim Square, tel: (212) 231-2121, fax: 231-2180. Complete with casino.

Pera Palace, 98 Meşrutiyet Caddesi, tel: (212) 251-4560, fax: 251-4089.

Built to accommodate passengers of the Orient Express; all the stars stayed here.

Yeşil Ev, 5 Kabasakal Sokak, Sultanahmet, tel: (212) 517-6785, fax: 517-6780. Ancient Ottoman town house with all mod cons and splendid old-world atmosphere.

MID-RANGE

Büyuk Londra, 117 Meşrutiyet Caddesi, tel: (212) 249-1025, fax: 245-0671. Built about the same time as Pera Palace, but less well preserved.

Hıdıv Kasrı, Hıdıv Kasrı, Çubuklu, tel: (216) 331-2651. Palace built for the ruler of Egypt at the turn of the century; out on the Asian shore.

Hotel Barın, 25 Fevziye Caddesi, tel: (212) 522-8426. Popular with Americans.

Hotel Opera, 38 İnönü Caddesi, Taksim, tel: (212) 143-5527. Serviceable hotel, with superb views out over the Bosphorus.

Hotel Zurich, 37 Harikzadeler Sokak, tel: (212) 512-2350. Modern, functional.

BUDGET

Berk Guest House, 27 Kutluğun Sokak, tel: (212) 516-9671.

Hotel München, 55 Gençtürk Caddesi, tel: (212) 526-5243.

Istanbul Plaza, Siraselviler Caddesi, 19 Aslanyatagi Sokak, Taksim, tel: (212) 245-3273. Inexpensive block with some fine views out over the Bosphorus.

Optimist Guesthouse, Hippodrome, tel: (212) 516-2398. Clean and comfortable.

Sultan Tourist Hostel, I2 Akbıyık Caddesi, Terbıyık Sokak, tel: (212) 515-9260.

WHERE TO EAT

Istanbul abounds with inexpensive kebab joints and street sellers hawking all kinds of exotic food. (However, you'd be well advised not to try the fresh mussels in hot weather, as these go off notoriously quickly.) Many moderate and inexpensively priced restaurants have their main dishes on display, so you can simply point out what you want. The variety is enormous, the standard generally excellent and alcohol is served.

For travellers tired of Turkish cuisine, world-famous fast-food outlets are available as well.

Bebek Ambassadeurs, 113 Cevdet Paşa Caddesi, Bebek, tel: (212) 263-3002. The place to see and be seen. Old-world sophistication, superb French and Turkish cuisine, with romantic views out over the Bosphorus.

Dort Mevsim, 509 Istiklâl Caddesi, tel: (212) 245-8941.

Köşem Cemal Restaurant, Kumkapi Meydanı, tel: (212) 520-1229. Great fresh seafood.

Revan Sheraton Hotel, Taksim Square, tel: (212) 231-2121. Luxury rooftop location, with romantic views to match the cuisine.

Taverna-Restaurant Sarniç, Soğukçeşme Sokak, tel: (212) 512-4291. Ottoman cuisine in atmospheric Roman cellars.

Üçler Restaurant, Kumkapı Square, no telephone booking.

Vitamin Restaurant, 16 Divan Yolu, tel: (212) 526-5086. Offers an excellent selection of inexpensive Middle Eastern dishes.

Pudding Shop, 24 Divan Yolu Caddesi. Has no telephone. World famous, an Istanbul institution since the 1960s.

TOURS AND EXCURSIONS

These are best arranged through a travel agent or your hotel. You are strongly advised against trying to book a tour by fax. There are a number of **city tours** which take in most of the main sites. There are also some excellent boat trips up the **Bosphorus** (especially at night), and to the Princes' Islands in the Sea of Marmara.

USEFUL CONTACTS

American Express, in the Hilton at Cumhuriyet Caddesi, tel: (212) 241-0248.

Atatürk Airport International, Enquiries Desk, tel: (212) 573-3500.

Cağaloğlu Hamam, Yerebatan Caddesi, tel: (212) 522-2424. Where Florence Nightingale, Kaiser Wilhelm II and Hercule Poirot sweated it out.

Çinar, 6 Nuruosmaniye Caddesi, for excellent kilims and carpets.

Imperial, 30 Divanyolu Caddesi, tel: (212) 513-9430. Alternatively, contact one of the **Ministry of Tourism** offices throughout the city:
• Hilton Hotel, tel: (212) 233-0592.
• Atatürk Airport, tel: (212) 673-4136.
• In the Old City, 3 Divan Yolu Caddesi, tel: (212) 522-4903.

Orion Tur, (tourist agency) 287/1 Halâskârgazi Caddesi, tel: (212) 241-8014.

Tourist Police, tel: (212) 627-4503.

ISTANBUL	J	F	M	A	M	J	J	A	S	O	N	D
AVERAGE TEMP. °F	46	47	51	60	69	77	82	82	76	68	59	51
AVERAGE TEMP. °C	8	9	11	16	21	25	28	28	24	20	15	11
HOURS OF SUN DAILY	3	5	7	6	8	7	9	10	8	6	7	4
RAINFALL in	4	4	3	2	2	1	1	1	2	3	4	5
RAINFALL mm	109	92	72	46	38	34	34	30	58	81	103	119
DAYS OF RAINFALL	18	14	14	9	8	6	4	4	7	11	14	18

3
Around The Sea Of Marmara

The northwestern part of the country, including the Sea of Marmara and the European plains, is often overlooked in favour of more glamorous spots, yet it contains a wider display of sights than almost anywhere else in Turkey and should not be missed.

This region witnessed the birth of the Ottoman Empire, whose first capital was at **Bursa**, just south of the Sea of Marmara. **Edirne**, up near the Greek border, was also a capital of the Ottoman Empire. In the 15th century it was renowned throughout the Middle East for its hundreds of splendid mosques and fountains, rivalled only by Baghdad.

At the western end of the Sea of Marmara are the **Dardanelles**, a narrow strip of water that has been of great strategic importance since ancient times. The northern shore of the Dardanelles is formed by the **Gallipoli Peninsula** (*Gelibolu*), scene of one of the most disastrous campaigns of World War I. The battlefields here remain largely undisturbed, and many a moving relic from the campaign is on view in the museum at **Çanakkale**.

The Sea of Marmara also contains some delightful, small islands, which are well worth visiting for their quaint fishing villages and lovely beaches. They can be reached by ferry from Erdek, on the edge of the **Kapıdağı Peninsula**. Another neglected spot is the historic walled town of **Iznik**, where artists produced the beautiful tiles that today adorn many of the finest mosques throughout Turkey.

DON'T MISS

*** Gallipoli Peninsula: site of the ill-fated Gallipoli Campaign of World War I.
*** Edirne: its mosques are among the finest in Turkey.
** Marmara Islands: delightful, small islands with fishing villages and beaches, very popular with Turkish holiday-makers.
** Bursa: first capital of the Ottoman Empire, renowned for its mosques and baths.
* Uludağ: one of Turkey's winter ski resorts, also good for summer hiking.

Opposite: *The marvellous dome and decorated ceiling of Edirne's impressive Selimiye Camii mosque.*

EDIRNE

If you drive west from Istanbul, down the E80 and
out across the rolling plains of European Turkey for
about 225km (140 miles), you will see the famous skyline
of Edirne, its domes and minarets rising dramatically
against the horizon.

Edirne lies on the **Meriç River**, quite close to the
Greek border. This ancient city was once proud
Adrianople, capital of **Thrace**, the province which covered European Turkey, northern Greece and part of
southern Bulgaria. It was founded by the ancient
Romans in the 2nd century AD, and named after
the **Emperor Hadrian**. Sultan Murat captured the city
in 1361, and for almost a century it remained the capital
of the steadily expanding Ottoman Empire. During the
15th century, Suleiman the Magnificent made Edirne
his summer capital, and it became one of the greatest
cities in the Middle East, rivalling beautiful and famous
Baghdad in its splendour, with almost 300 mosques
and 100 public fountains.

Selimiye Camii ★★

Many of the old mosques are still standing. The finest is the Selimiye Camii, built
in the 16th century by a then aged **Mimar
Sinan**, greatest mosque architect of all
time, who considered this his master-
piece. It was built for **Selim the Grim**,
and according to local legend has 999
windows, because Selim didn't want to
tempt fate by having a thousand. Its four
minarets are over 70m (230ft) high; only
those in Mecca are higher.

Inside, the superb high dome is
even wider than that of Aya Sofya in
Istanbul. Its surface is inscribed with
delicate calligraphy, offering prayers to
Allah. The sultan's lodge is probably the
only one in Turkey with a window
opening towards Mecca.

Left: Musicians look on as eager competitors line up for the Kirkpinar Wrestling Championships.
Opposite: Edirne used to be one of the greatest cities in the Middle East; it's still a lively centre.

The Old Town *

Another mosque worth visiting is the **Muradiye Camii**, built by Murat for the **Mevlevi Dervishes** (*see* p. 98), which lies a short walk northeast of the city centre. The ancient blue Iznik tiles that decorate its interior are amongst the finest in the land. Just across **Dilaver Bey** (central park) from the Selimiye Camii you come to the **Bedesten**, one of the oldest covered markets in Turkey, selling mostly household goods. Its structure consists of over a dozen vaulted chambers, which do wonders for amplifying the hubbub of the traders below. Just west of the Bedesten lies the ancient **Kale Içı** quarter, its grid-patterned streets and old, terraced houses dating from Byzantine times.

Edirne Saray *

Follow the walk east along the river to **Saray Içı**, the island supporting the rather disappointing ruins of the Sultan's Palace, which centuries ago rivalled the Topkapı in Istanbul. Nearby is the stadium where the **Kirkpinar** (oiled wrestling) Championships are held.

Also worth a visit is the **Museum of Turkish and Islamic Arts**, just east of the Selimiye Camii, which has a wide range of historic exhibits, including some excellent ceramic tiles. But pride of place belongs to a portrait gallery of previous Kirkpinar champions. Open 10:00–14:00 Monday, 08:00–17:30 Tuesday–Sunday.

OILED WRESTLING

Edirne is famous as the venue for the Kirkpinar Wrestling Championships held annually in late June to early July, depending on Ramadan. Contestants cover their bodies from head to foot in olive oil, and wear unique leather pants. The wrestling contests have few apparent rules. The loser is the first contestant to collapse or be pinned to the ground. The championships attract thousands of contestants from all over Turkey, and the winner achieves great prestige for his region or village.

Above: *The toll of war –*
World War I gravestones
at Gallipoli.

GALLIPOLI PENINSULA
Çanakkale *

About 190km (120 miles) south of Edirne, down E87, you come to Çanakkale. This somewhat drab but strategically placed town lies at the entrance to the Dardanelles.

Çanakkale makes an ideal base for visiting the Gallipoli battlefields on the **Gelibolu Peninsula**. The local **Army and Navy Museum** contains a great number of fascinating relics from the campaign, including the pocket watch which saved Atatürk's life by stopping a bullet.

Also of interest is the **Archaeological Museum**, which displays many finds unearthed at Ancient Troy, 27km (17 miles) away. Unfortunately this doesn't include any of the major discoveries, which are today housed either in the national museums or in Germany. To make up for this, the museum has a small but superb collection of ancient coins, ranging from primitive pre-Hellenic groats to magnificent Ottoman sovereigns. Open 08:00–12:00 and 13:00–16:30 daily.

Gökçeada *

This is the ancient *Imbros* mentioned by **Homer**. Ferries to the island run on a regular basis from the village of **Kabatepe** on the Gelibolu Peninsula (in summer) and Çanakkale (in winter). You'll need a military permit (obtainable in Çanakkale) before you set out to explore Gökçeada's 15th-century castle ruin and some fine but remote beaches.

The World War I Battlefields ***

In 1915 **Winston Churchill** hatched a daring plan to resupply the ailing Russian forces and knock Turkey out of the war. The British and French fleets were to force their way up the Dardanelles and bombard Istanbul until

---

THE LEGEND OF HERO AND LEANDER

In ancient times the Dardanelles, known then as the Hellespont, was the site of one of the most romantic of Ancient Greek legends. Each night Leander would swim across this treacherous strait for a tryst with his lover, the priestess Hero. She would always light a lantern in her tower to guide him. One night a storm blew out the lantern, and before Hero could relight it, Leander lost his way and was drowned. When his body was discovered the next morning, an anguished Hero flung herself into the waves to be reunited with her dead lover.

the Turks capitulated, but the plan turned into a fiasco. Most of the Allied warships were stopped by the batteries guarding the entrance to the **Dardanelles** at Çanakkale; the few that managed to battle past, fell victim to mines. Churchill decided to try a different tack: the Allies would invade the Gallipoli Peninsula and take the Dardanelles.

On 25 April 1915, British, French and ANZAC (Australia and New Zealand Army Corps) troops invaded. The beaches were narrow, bordered by steeply rising terrain – and the Turks were waiting. A narrow beachhead was established and remained under constant bombardment from the Turks, but the Allies dug in. Their **trenches,** very often only 20m (65ft) from the Turkish lines, are still visible amid the fragrant pines.

The Allies persisted for over eight months, by which time they had lost over 250,000 men. The Turks (led by their ablest young commander **Lt-Col Mustafa Kemal**, who had inspired his men with many acts of selfless heroism) had sustained similar tragic losses. In January 1916, the Allies finally withdrew, having achieved absolutely nothing. Churchill was forced to resign in disgrace.

Begin your tour of the battlefields at the **Kabatepe Information Centre**, with its stirring exhibit of photos and relics from the campaign. Some 30 **cemeteries** serve as a reminder of the atrocities of war. You can also visit the beaches and trenches, where poignant remains of the war linger on in the form of rusted bully-beef tins and spent bullets.

The best, most informative way to take in the sights is to join one of the day-long **tours** which start from Çanakkale. These are conducted by guides whose intimate knowledge of the battlefields and the surrounding area brings history to life.

ANZAC DAY
The Gallipoli Campaign saw some exceptionally brave fighting by the Australians and New Zealanders who made up the **ANZAC** troops. Many thousands of them lost their lives here. ANZAC Day is a public holiday in both **Australia** and **New Zealand** to commemorate the fallen in both World Wars. It is held on 25 April, the day of the first Gallipoli landings.

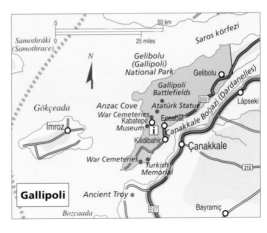

Marmara Denizi
(Sea of Marmara)

Marmara
Ekinlik Ad.   Marmara Ad.
Avşa Ad.   KAPIDAĞI
PENINSULA
Paşalimanı Ad.
Erdek   BANDIRMA
Kuşcenneti
National Park
Kuş Gölü

MUSTAFA KEMAL

The Turkish troops who
fought at Gallipoli were
composed largely of ill-
trained and ill-equipped
peasant recruits. They were
led by Lt-Col Mustafa Kemal,
undoubtedly Turkey's
greatest military genius.
Kemal believed in inspiring his
troops with acts of personal
bravery, often directing his
men in full view of enemy
guns. Later Mustafa Kemal
went on to become the first
president of modern Turkey,
adopting the name Atatürk,
Father of the Turks.

MARMARA ISLANDS

These are the small, pleasant islands which lie at
the southwestern end of the Sea of Marmara. They
can be reached by regular **ferry service** from **Erdek,**
on the south Marmara coast, and also by direct ferry
access from **Istanbul,** during the summer. There are
over half a dozen islands, but only the four largest ones
are permanently inhabited. The Marmara Islands are
very popular with Turkish tourists during the **summer,**
but they seldom become overrun, except during
weekends at the height of the season.

Marmara Island is the largest of the group and has
a length of about 16km (10 miles). Some 2500 years ago
this was a flourishing colony of the Ionian-Greek city of
Miletus, whose ruins lie 300km (190 miles) away on the
southwestern coast of mainland Turkey. Marmara
Island was famous for its marble (*marmara* is Greek for
marble, hence the colony's name) and there is still a
mine in the north of the island. The main coastal village,
also called Marmara, has steep, picturesque streets,
and there are several good beaches and swimming
coves along the coast.

Avşa Island, which lies to the southwest, also has
some very fine beaches and is famous for its wine.
Paşalimanı is more wooded and remote, and **Ekinlik**
is even more remote, with just one tiny village.

Right: *Marmara Island
can be a haven of tranquility,
though in summer it receives
a good number of visitors.*
Opposite: *The presence of
Sultan Mehmet I is still
felt in Bursa, not least
in his Green Mausoleum.*

BURSA

This sprawling city lies just 20km (12½ miles) inland, at the southeastern end of the Sea of Marmara. Nowadays it is renowned for producing cars, and is sometimes called the Detroit of Turkey. Yet it guards many remains of its long illustrious past.

The site of Bursa is said to have been chosen in the 3rd century BC by **Hannibal**, the famous Carthaginian general. Later it was occupied by the **Romans**, and then by the **Crusaders**. Finally, in 1326 it was taken by the Turks and became the first capital of the expanding Ottoman Empire. Ever since then, Bursa has been held in particular affection.

Bursa **knives** are renowned throughout Turkey and are on sale all over the city. Bursa is also renowned for its many baths, the most famous of which are the **Yeni Kaplica**, which were built nearly 500 years ago on a site dating back to Roman times.

Yeşil Cami **

The town of Bursa has several superb mosques, the finest of which is the **Green Mosque** (Yeşil Cami), which was built in the early 15th century by Sultan Mehmet I, who so loved it that he lived in it. Open 08:30–12:00, 13:00–17:30 daily.

TURKISH BATHS

On entering the baths you divest yourself of your clothes in a cubicle and proceed to the steaming room, clad in a towel. Here you relax on a large, hot, circular stone platform. This process opens the pores, and is extremely tranquilizing and soothing. Here you can also subject yourself to a vigorous traditional massage. Afterwards you enter the warming and cooling rooms, where you douse yourself alternately with hot and cold water, which is both relaxing and exhilarating. Many spend hours in the *hamam*, taking beer or tea, or even having a snooze. Afterwards you will feel wonderfully clean and revitalized. A visit to the baths costs little and is a quintessentially Turkish experience.

Above: *Picturesque street in an old quarter of Bursa.*
Opposite: *The town of Iznik is renowned for its marvellous blue-green tiles.*

IZNIK'S MOMENTS OF GREATNESS

In AD325 Iznik was the site of the first **Ecumenical Council.** Here, elders of the Christian Church decided upon the **Nicaean Creed** which outlined the fundamental tenets of Christian belief. The second council was also held here, 400 years later, under the Byzantine **Empress Irene**. This time rituals were formalized into the structure that the Greek church still adheres to today. After the sacking of Constantinople in 1204, Iznik briefly became the capital of the Byzantine Empire.

Opposite, you can see his magnificent tomb, the **Green Mausoleum**. The mosque was badly damaged by a major earthquake in 1855, but has since been restored. Of particular interest is the fine marble carving around the main door. This was the first mosque to reflect a truly Turkish style. Previous builders had followed Persian designs, but here we see evolving the style which was to achieve its final glory in the works of Sinan and the great mosques of Istanbul.

Museum of Turkish and Islamic Art ★★
Just east of Yeşil Cami lies the **Museum of Turkish and Islamic Art.** Open 08:00–12:00, 13:00–17:00 Tuesday–Sunday, 10:00–13:00 Monday. Of particular interest here is the large display of **Karagöz shadow puppets**. Karagöz puppet plays, said to have originated in Bursa, once appeared in travelling shows throughout the Ottoman Empire. Indeed, they remained popular in the Balkans until 50 years ago.

The origin of these plays, which are reminiscent of the British 'Punch and Judy' shows, has its own legend. According to this tale, comical Karagöz and his partner, Hacıvat, fell foul of Sultan Orhan, because they distracted fellow workers building the **Orhan Gazi Camii** with their antics. In anger, he ordered to have them beheaded, but later came to miss the funny pair and promptly ordered their return as shadow characters, thus ensuring their immortality.

Ulu Cami ★★
Another mosque that shouldn't be missed is the Ulu Cami, which stands in the town centre and dates from the reign of **Sultan Yıldırım Beyazit I** in the late 14th century. It has no less than 20 domes, and the interior contains a pleasant pool and some fine woodwork. This mosque is known especially for its *mihrab* (carved prayer niche indicating the direction of Mecca).

Uluabat Gölü *

About 40km (25 miles) west of Bursa, off the main road to **Bandırma**, lies the lake of Uluabat Gölü. Around it there are several picturesque Ottoman villages, like the little fishing village of **Gölyazı** at the eastern end of the lake.

Uludağ *

This mountain, at the centre of a **national park** just south of Bursa, provides a spectacular backdrop to the city and is one of its main attractions. Uludağ rises to over 2500m (8200ft) and for much of the year is covered in snow. In winter there is a **ski resort** near the top, whose gentle slopes are popular with weekend skiers. In summer you can go **hiking** along well-marked trails in the woods, or up to the lakes near the summit. The mountain can be reached from **Teferüç** in south Bursa, where there is a **cable-car** which takes you up to over 1600m (5200ft).

IZNIK

This market town, lying approximately 80km (50 miles) northeast of Bursa on the shore of the scenic lake **Iznik Gölü**, is surrounded by ancient city walls. The ruined old church is renowned for its splendid frescoes and mosaics which date from Byzantine times. The main mosque, Yeşil Cami, dates from the late 15th century.

Opposite Yeşil Cami, the **Iznik Museum** contains some fine examples of the blue-green **tiles** for which this town was once famous. There are also interesting, well-labelled classical and Byzantine relics, all of which were excavated locally.

The city itself was probably founded around 3000 years ago. It was originally known as Nicaea, named after the wife of one of Alexander the Great's generals and was the site of the first **Ecumenical Council** of the Christian Church in 325 under the Emperor Constantine.

BURSA SILK

In late Roman times, silk was an expensive luxury. It had to be imported all the way from **China** along the **Silk Road**, and the Chinese jealously guarded the secret of making silk. Eventually, a group of Nestorians succeeded in smuggling out **silk worms** in hollow canes. The caterpillars were brought to Bursa, which established itself as the new centre of the silk trade.

Around the Sea of Marmara at a Glance

BEST TIMES TO VISIT

This region can be cold and wet in **winter**, but there is good **skiing** (by Turkish standards) on the slopes of Uludağ, just south of Bursa. Spring is still cool, but the flowers are superb. Summer is sunny, but can be hot at midday, and the beaches become a favourite haunt for most. **Autumn** is an excellent time to visit, with long **sunny** days.

GETTING THERE

There are internal flights from Istanbul to Bursa. Ferries run from Istanbul to the Marmara Islands in summer. There are regular bus and dolmuş services from Istanbul to Edirne, Çanakkale and Iznik. Istanbul is also linked to Edirne by rail.

GETTING AROUND

The main towns and places of interest in this region are connected by regular bus and dolmuş services, with the exception of the Marmara Islands. These are linked by ferry services which run from Erdek on the Kapıdağ Peninsula. There is also a ferry across the Dardanelles from Çanakkale. All these ferries take cars.

WHERE TO STAY

Bursa
LUXURY
Hotel Dılmen, Murat Caddesi 20, Bursa, tel: (24) 36-6114. Large modern hotel at the western end of town in the Çekirge district (famous for its thermal springs). Fine views from here and the hotel has its own thermal baths.

MID-RANGE
Ada Palas, 21 Murat Caddesi, tel: (24) 36-1650. At the Kültür Park end of town, complete with its own thermal pool. Less expensive than many in this district.
Hotel Dıkmen, Fevzi Çamak, Caddesi 78, Bursa, tel: (24) 21499. A friendly hotel right in the centre of town. Handles tours, used to speaking English and dealing with tourist requests.
Otel Çamlibel, 71 Inebey Caddesi, tel: (24) 112-2565. Slightly gloomy, old-style atmosphere, but excellent value for money, and right in the heart of town. It is best to book ahead as this is a popular spot.
Termal Hotel Gönlü Ferah, 1 Murat Caddesi 24, Çekirge, tel: (24) 36-2700. The best rooms here have superb views out over the valley. Old grand hotel atmosphere.

Çanakkale
MID-RANGE
Akol, Kordonboyu, Çanakkale, tel: (196) 79456. Moderately priced hotel situated right on the seafront, with lovely views out over the Dardanelles.
Grand Truva Oteli, Kayserili Ahmet Paşa Caddesi, tel: (196) 11024. The older section of the hotel has rooms with views out over the Dardanelles, the landward-side rooms tend to be smarter.
Tusan Güzelyalı, Güzelyalı, tel: (1973) 8210. Pleasant holiday hotel by the beach, ten-minute drive south of Çanakkale on the way to Troy. It has a nearby beach and is ideal for children.

Edirne
MID-RANGE
Hotel Rüstempaşa Kervansaray, Iki Kapılı Han Caddesi. Built in the 16th century for the vizier of Suleiman the Magnificent. Most historic hotel in town.
Sultan Oteli, 170 Talat Paşa Caddesi, tel: (181) 11372. In the heart of town by the tourist office and all the main sights. Friendly service; English spoken by many staff.

WHERE TO EAT

Bursa
Hacıc Bey, Ünlü Caddesi, Heykel 7, tel: (224) 21-4615. No credit cards. Great favourite with the locals, so be sure to get here early (for lunch or dinner). Hardly an atmospheric spot, but the clientele is very friendly, and the food is highly authentic.
Kebapcı Iskenderoğlu, Ünlü Caddesi 7, tel: (224) 21-4615.

Around the Sea of Marmara at a Glance

They say the original Bursa Kebab was invented in a restaurant on this site. The locals still reckon they serve the best one in town. Inexpensive, and the decor is rather cafeteria-like.

Selçuk Restaurant, Kültür Parki İçi, tel: (224) 20-9696. Excellent menu includes Turkish and several local specialities. In summer you can dine out on a pleasant terrace. Right by the park.

Çanakkale

Bizzim Entellektüel, on the seafront, no booking. The name means 'our intellectuals', but it's a popular spot with all sorts. Terrace outside overlooks the Dardanelles.

Restaurant Dardanel, on the seafront, no booking. Large, highly popular spot with consistently good local cuisine.

Edirne

Aile Restaurant, Saraçlar Caddesi, Belediye İş Hanı. No booking. Upstairs restaurant which serves good local cuisine. The waiters are friendly and many speak English. Don't be put off by the rather drab exterior.

Cafe M, Saraçlar Caddesi, Vakıf İş Hanı, tel: (181) 23448. Upstairs café which also serves good light meals. Just the place for a snack after visiting the nearby sights.

TOURS AND EXCURSIONS

By far the best tours of the **Gallipoli Battlefields** are organized by **Troy-Anzac Tours** (*see* Useful Contacts below). They run 3-hour tours, accompanied by guides who are knowledgeable and friendly. These guides are often English language teachers from Istanbul taking a break. They are willing to answer all kinds of questions about the battlefields and the campaign, and are even able to advise on visiting other places in Turkey.

In Bursa the **No 1 bus** links all the main tourist sights in town. Its route starts at the Emir Sultan Cami at the eastern end of town, and ends at the baths in Çekirge suburb. There are no tours as such of the **Marmara Islands**. However, the Tourist Information Office in Erdek (*see* Useful Contacts below) has details of ferry timetables to the islands. With the aid of these it is possible to plan your own round-trip.

Skiing at Uludağ:

Though the standard of skiing in Turkey is not com-

parable to that in Alpine areas, a weekend at Uludağ makes for a refreshing break, and lies within a convenient travelling distance from Istanbul. All the necessary equipment can be hired at local hotels. There are several downhill runs that are quite good. They are usually open for about four months, from November to early in March. One recommended option is to spend the night in **Bursa** and catch the local transport up to the slopes each day. This gives the traveller a chance to experience a little of the nightlife as well.

USEFUL CONTACTS

Tourist Information Office, Hükümet Caddesi 54, Erdek, (on the Kapıdağı Peninsula), for ferry timetables to the Marmara Islands.

Troy-Anzac Tours, Yali Caddese, Çanakkale, tel: (196) 15047, for comprehensive tours of the Gallipoli battlefields.

Turkish Airlines, Türk Hava Yolu, Çakir Hamam Temiz Caddesi 16/B, Bursa, tel: (24) 21-1167.

BURSA	J	F	M	A	M	J	J	A	S	O	N	D
AVERAGE TEMP. °F	47	48	51	60	69	78	81	81	76	69	60	52
AVERAGE TEMP. °C	9	9	11	17	22	24	27	27	23	22	17	11
HOURS OF SUN DAILY	4	5	8	8	7	9	10	11	8	6	6	4
RAINFALL in	4	4	3	2	2	1	1	1	2	3	4	5
RAINFALL mm	102	90	71	41	38	35	34	31	55	80	103	120
DAYS OF RAINFALL	16	14	14	9	8	6	4	4	7	11	14	18

4
The Aegean Coast

Turkey has over 500km (300 miles) of Aegean coast-line, as well as a number of nearby islands. Much of the scenery here is typically **Mediterranean**: little inlets and coves, clear aquamarine sea and lovely, sandy beaches, overlooked by rocky slopes and olive groves. Like most of the Aegean, this is serious holiday territory. There aren't many utterly unspoilt spots – though a few still persist, as long as you're willing to venture off the beaten track.

Modern resorts such as **Kuşadası**, **Bodrum** and **Ayvalık** are popular with the sun 'n' fun set and the nightclubs here are as hectic as any on the Costa Brava.

Yet there's a lot more to this coast than sunburn and strobe lights. **Pergamum** and **Ephesus** are two of the finest ancient cities you'll see anywhere. Amid the extensive ruins and ancient streets, many buildings, temples and amphitheatres have remained virtually unchanged for 2000 years. Less well preserved, but even more evocative, is ancient **Troy,** where legendary Homeric ghosts haunt the fallen stones.

Another natural beauty is to be found inland at **Pamukkale**. Here spectacular terraced pools, formed by crystallized mineral salts, spill down the mountain-side in suspended animation.

The main city in this region is **Izmir** (ancient Smyrna), which is now a thriving seaport and the second largest city in Turkey. There are several good resorts within easy reach of Izmir along the western peninsula which forms the Gulf of Izmir.

Opposite: *The historic town of Bodrum is a favourite port of call on the Aegean Coast.*

NORTHERN AEGEAN COAST
Troy **

South of the Dardanelles the main road turns inland, and after a few miles you arrive at the ruins of Ancient Troy. As they stand, these are hardly the most impressive legacy from the ancient world, yet the rich legend they evoke easily makes up for this. Troy has atmosphere. We know exactly what happened here over 3000 years ago. It's all there in Homer's *Iliad*.

Today you can still see the gate through which the Trojans dragged their wooden horse. Excavations have proved that no less than nine cities existed on this site – the first dating from the Early Bronze Age over 5500 years ago.

The present site beckons with a rather awkward reconstruction of the legendary wooden horse out on the parking lot. More interesting is the small house nearby, where **Schliemann** lived while conducting the excavations. Inside you can see his somewhat primitive working equipment, and photos of his wife wearing the famous jewelled ornaments he discovered.

Amid the extensive ruins you can see the remains of the city walls, as well as those of a theatre and council chamber. Sadly, there is no real museum on the site: the fabulous treasures unearthed by Schliemann are now retained in museums in Berlin and St Petersburg.

Below: *Schliemann's trench, where the great German archaeologist conducted his dig at the site of ancient Troy.*

Bozcaada **

South of Troy you can catch a boat across to Bozcaada, the second of Turkey's Aegean islands. This is officially a **military area** and you'll first need to get a pass in Çanakkale. The island is only about 12km (8 miles) in length, and has just one small town of cobbled streets overlooked by picturesque

Ottoman balconies. Above the rooftops stands the imposing ruin of a 500-year-old **Venetian castle**. The island's history goes back to Homeric times – this was where the Ancient Greek fleet hid, after they had left the wooden horse outside the walls of Troy. Bozcaada is hardly undiscovered, but it has yet to suffer the rigours and heavy demands of modern tourism. The island is justly renowned for its pleasant white wine.

Back on the mainland, the road continues south to the coast, with some fine views out over the blue waters of the **Gulf of Edremit**, and follows the shoreline to the popular seaside resort of Ayvalık.

Aegean Coast

Ayvalık **

Like most such spots, Ayvalık first began attracting tourists because of its exceptional beauty and comfortable amenities. And despite the commercial efforts of the villa builders and the souvenir sellers these remain largely intact and unspoilt. Ayvalık is tucked into a pleasant bay, with some good **beaches** nearby and half a dozen small **islands** around, all of which you can visit by boat. From the road south there are views out over the sea towards the Greek island of **Lesbos**. There are a number of nice beaches along this stretch of coast, and some minor classical ruins off the road at **Melene** and **Canae**.

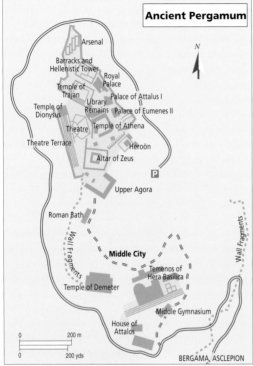

Ancient Pergamum

Arsenal

Barracks and
Hellenistic Tower

Royal
Palace

Temple of
Trajan

Library
Remains

Palace of Attalus I

Palace of Eumenes II

Temple of
Dionysus

Theatre

Temple of Athena

Theatre Terrace

Heroön

Altar of Zeus

Upper Agora

Roman Bath

Wall Fragments

Middle City

Wall Fragments

Temenos of
Hera Basilica

Temple of Demeter

Middle Gymnasium

House of
Attalos

0   200 m

0   200 yds

BERGAMA, ASCLEPION

PERGAMUM (BERGAMA)

About 36km (22 miles) south down the coastal road from Ayvalık, you turn off inland to reach Bergama. If you go by bus, it is wise to make sure that it goes all the way, or you will be dropped off 8km (5 miles) from the archaeological site on the outskirts of town. On the hillside above modern Bergama stands ancient **Pergamum**, whose ruins rate among the finest in the entire Mediterranean region and their situation, high on the bluff overlooking the surrounding plain, is as striking as any found on the Aegean seaboard.

The original settlement was founded by the Greeks as early as the 8th century BC, but it was to be another four centuries before the city rose to prominence, as a result of stolen treasure. After the death of **Alexander the Great,** his general, **Lysimachus**, left Alexander's entire fortune in the charge of his trusted eunuch **Philetarus**, while he himself set off to campaign in Syria. When Lysimachus was killed, Philetarus refused to surrender the 10,000 gold talents he was guarding, and instead started the building project which established Pergamum's greatness.

During the ensuing centuries Pergamum extended its territory, until by 190BC it ruled an empire covering almost half of Asia Minor. The city developed into one of the main cultural centres of the Ancient World, with superb temples and public buildings.

The **library** at Pergamum became second only to the great library at Alexandria. Indeed, the rivalry between these two bastions of classical learning soon became so fierce that the Alexandrians even blocked the export of papyrus from Egypt to Pergamum. Nowadays nothing but a few stones are left of this great library.

The Acropolis **

Fortunately, many of Pergamum's fine buildings have survived the ravages of time and conquest, among them the slender marble columns of **Trajan's Temple**. But the best reminder of the sheer size and splendour of ancient Pergamum is its superb **theatre**, whose terraced rows of seats are carved in a great arc into the hillside overlooking the valley below. In its heyday this theatre seated over 10,000 spectators and even today it retains splendid acoustics – try it out yourself. The river below was dammed then, creating an artificial lake on which naval galleons, manned by hundreds of gladiators and galley slaves, would engage in bloody battles.

The greatest building of all at Pergamum was the **Temple of Zeus**, which is mentioned in the Bible's Book of Revelations as 'the place where Satan has his altar'. All that remains today is the altar's foundation, which nonetheless makes an impressive sight.

> **THE FACE THAT LAUNCHED A THOUSAND SHIPS**
>
> According to Homer's *Iliad*, Paris abducted Helen, the beautiful wife of King Menelaus of Sparta, and carried her back to Troy. The outraged Menelaus summoned his Greek allies Odysseus, Achilles, Agamemnon, and together with a large army they sailed across the Aegean in 1000 ships to besiege Troy. The siege dragged on quite unsuccessfully for years (and dozens of verses of Homer), until the Greeks pretended to give up and sailed away, leaving behind a rather large wooden horse. The joyously relieved Trojans dragged the curious wooden effigy into the city. That night, soldiers concealed inside its belly slipped out and opened the city gates to admit the Greek army, which had returned under the cover of darkness.

Left: *The ancient amphitheatre of Pergamum sits high above the modern town of Bergama.*
Opposite: *Pergamum's Trajan's Temple retains its delicate marble columns.*

A NEW FORM OF PAPER

In the Ancient World, books were written on **papyrus** made of the bullrushes from the Nile Delta. When the jealous Egyptians boycotted the supply of papyrus to the rival library of Pergamum, librarians here were unable to produce any further scrolls. To overcome this hindrance, a new way of treating animal hides was invented. The new material became known as *pergamene*, which is the origin of our word parchment.

The **Acropolis** lies at the end of the curving road which ascends for 5km (3 miles) from the modern town. All the main monuments are within easy walking distance of one another, but if you wish you can also explore the remains of the **Gymnasium** (school) and the **Lower Agora** (market place) further down the hill towards Bergama. These tend to be less crowded and can easily be reached in 10 minutes. Open 09:00–12:00 and 13:00–19:00 daily.

The Archaeological Museum ★★

The modern town of Bergama is rather disappointing after the glories of ancient Pergamum. However, it does contain an interesting Archaeological Museum on the main street, on the left after you enter town. It contains a varied collection of more recent local finds. These may not match the pillaged masterpieces, now on show in Berlin's Pergamum Museum, but there is some interesting portraiture, including a bust of Socrates and a statue of the Emperor Hadrian. The little outside café here is a delight, with tables created from ancient pillar segments. Open 9:00–12.00 and 13:00–17:00 daily.

Below: *A superb Roman statue depicting the Emperor Hadrian stands on display in Bergama's Archaeological Museum.*

The Asceplion ★

On the other side of the valley from the main Acropolis, 20 minutes' walk west of the Archaeological Museum, are the ruins of the Asclepion. This temple dates from the 4th century BC and is dedicated to Asclepius, the son of Apollo, who was the Greek god of Healing. (His emblem, a snake curled about a winged staff, still adorns many a modern chemist shop.) The Asclepion at Pergamum was one of the great healing centres of the Ancient World. Medical science, then in its infancy, was a blend of quackery and primitive cures. Many rituals were conducted on this site, one of which involved walking through a tunnel (still in existence), while a physician whispered a cure in the patient's ear. Yet the techniques developed here were to produce the first great physician in Western history: Galen.

IZMIR

Izmir is Turkey's main Mediterranean port, an important **NATO** headquarters, and the third largest city in the country, after Istanbul and Ankara. The first thing you notice upon arrival, especially in summer, is the heat and the noise. Nowadays it isn't an instantly attractive spot, though in ancient times it was said to be so beautiful that the Roman Emperor Marcus Aurelius burst into tears when he heard that it had been flattened by an earthquake.

Almost nothing remains from this era, and not entirely due to earthquakes. After Turkey's defeat in World War I, the Greeks mounted an invasion from across the Aegean, which soon turned into a fiasco. As the Turks advanced, retreating remnants of the Greek army joined thousands of Greek civilians who had been living in the Anatolian hinterland, as they fled towards Izmir. The city became a chaos of desperate refugees scrambling to get passage on outbound boats. A massacre ensued, the city caught fire and burned to the ground. Over 30,000 people lost their lives.

As with so many ancient cities, the bustle and exhaust fumes of modern streets help to mask a history which contains unimaginable horrors. The difference in Izmir is that these took place within the lifetime of some of the old men you can see today, sitting in the shade and fingering their worry beads.

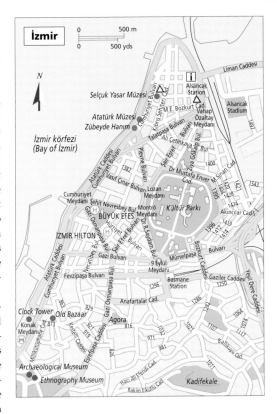

İzmir

0 500 m
0 500 yds

N

Liman Caddesi

Selçuk Yasar Müzesi

Alsancak Station
Alsancak Stadium

Atatürk Müzesi
Zübeyde Hanım

M.E. Bozkurt Cad.
Vahap
Özaltay Meydanı

İzmir körfezi
(Bay of İzmir)

Pievne Bulvarı

Dr Mustafa Enver Cad.

Cumhuriyet Meydanı
Şehit Nevresbey Bul
Montrö Meydanı
Kültür Parkı

BÜYÜK EFES

İZMİR HILTON

Gazi Bulvarı
Mürselpaşa Bul
Bulvarı

Fevzipaşa Bulvarı
9 Eylül Meydanı
Basmane Station
Gaziler Caddesi

Anafartalar Cad.

Clock Tower Old Bazaar
Konak Meydanı
Agora

Archaeological Museum
Ethnography Museum
Kadifekale

THE DISCOVERY OF PERGAMUM

Pergamum was rediscovered by accident in 1871. When **Karl Humann**, the German engineer in charge of building the Istanbul–Izmir railway, ran out of stone, he sent his labourers into the nearby hills. When they returned with a number of exquisitely carved blocks of marble, he set off to search for the source and found the ruins of one of the ancient world's greatest cities.

The Archaeological and Ethnographic Museums *

These museums, open 09:00–12:00 and 13:00–17:00 daily, lie five minutes' walk south of the **Karşiyaka ferry terminal**,

The **Archaeological Museum** contains finds from the Izmir region, along with a pleasant Roman mosaic and some fine classical statues, such as a 2nd-century impression of Poseidon and Demeter, a statue of a Roman Priest and a little bronze Runner.

The **Ethnography Museum** across the road is located in a former late-Ottoman hospital. Reconstructed dwellings and old photos give a good idea of what Izmir was like before 1922. There's also an intriguing reconstruction of an **Ottoman chemist's shop**.

The Bazaar **

Some 400m (438yd) north of the museums lies the bazaar quarter, the largest in the country outside Istanbul. Here you'll find the best **jewellers**. This, and the area just to the south, are best for **leatherwear** (from jackets to shoes). Be sure to explore down the back alleyways, where you'll find vendors hawking everything from school exercise books and obscure fuses to live ducks.

Just east of the Bazaar lies the ancient Agora, originally built in the 4th century BC by Alexander the Great, and destroyed twice by earthquakes during the classical era.

Kadifekale *

High above the city stands Kadifekale (which in Turkish means 'velvet fortress'). At night, this ruined 500-year-old castle is floodlit, making it an impressive landmark. But the best time to visit this site is during the late afternoon, when you can watch the beautiful sunset over the city, and hear the muezzins calling from the minarets. Regular dolmuşes run from Konak by the waterfront.

GREATEST PHYSICIAN OF THE ANCIENT WORLD

Galen was born about 129BC, and underwent his medical apprenticeship at the Asclepion in Pergamum. He rapidly achieved such renown for his healing skills that he was invited to Rome to treat the emperor. Galen's treatises on medical practice were so profound, that they became the standard works and were to remain so until the end of the Middle Ages, 1500 years after they had been written. He was the first to discover that arteries carry blood, not air as had been thought until then. He also dissected pigs and Barbary apes to learn about anatomy.

ÇEŞME PENINSULA

If you wish to escape the heat of Izmir, you can always head for Çeşme at the end of the peninsula that forms the Gulf of Izmir. Along here there are many pleasant beaches and attractive small resorts.

SARDIS

Inland, on the road to **Salihli**, are the ruins of ancient Sardis. This was the city once ruled by **Croesus**, the richest king in the ancient world, whose name has now become a byword for opulence. In ancient times, tiny particles of alluvial gold washed down the streams and rivers from the mountains here, and were collected in sheepskins by the **Lydians**. It is thought that this practice gave rise to the legend of the **Golden Fleece**, which was sought by **Jason and the Argonauts**.

EPHESUS (EFES)

The site of ancient Ephesus lies 16km (10 miles) northeast of the popular resort of **Kuşadası**. In the view of many experts Ephesus is the best preserved of all ancient classical cities, outshining even Pompeii. Although much of the city is in ruins, there are enough buildings and streets still standing to give a good idea of what it must have been like to have lived here 2000 years ago.

THE MUEZZIN'S CALL

One of the most atmospheric characteristics of the Muslim Middle East is the muezzin's call. Five times a day you will hear the muezzin's strident ululating call ringing out over the rooftops from a nearby minaret, summoning the faithful to prayer. The first sounds at daybreak, and is particularly evocative in the dreamlike transition from dark to light. Like it or not, this is one of the few experiences a visitor to the Middle East is unlikely to forget.

Opposite: *Izmir's modern town hall occupies a commanding position along the waterfront.*
Left: *The picturesque harbour at Çeşme offers escape from the bustling and hot town of Izmir.*

WHAT'S IN A NAME

Nowadays, a person of great wealth is often said to be 'as rich as Croesus'. Croesus was once the fabulously wealthy King of Sardis. Just south of Izmir is the winding river Menderes, which in classical times used to be called the Meander, from which our term 'meander' derives. King Tantalus of Magnesia was doomed to *Hades* (hell) for murdering his sons. Here a delicious banquet was laid out before him, but each time he leaned forward to quench his thirst and still his hunger, it receded just beyond his reach, hence the word 'tantalize'.

Around the end of the 1st century BC, Ephesus had a population of almost a third of a million and was one of the main ports along the Aegean coast. Then the sea began to recede across the flat plain of the **Menderes River** (this process has continued so that the ruins of Ephesus are now several kilometres away from the sea). The silting up of the port spelt the city's ruin, and it was ultimately abandoned. However, for us this disaster was a blessing. No invading army wished to waste its time destroying a deserted city, thereby preserving its ruins for generations to come. The finest of all is undoubtedly the **Library of Celsus**, with its delicately pillared façade and intricately carved interior. The nearby **Arcadian Way**, which is lined with columns, once led down to the sea. Also not to be missed are the **Lower Agora** and the 25,000-seat **theatre** carved into the mountain, which are at the inland end of the Arcadian Way. On a slightly less elevated plane but equally interesting is the nearby row of ancient Public Lavatories, and the inevitable Bordello.

Meryemana ★

St Paul as well as the evangelists St Luke and St John spent time here and **St Luke** is thought to have paid several visits to Ephesus. Outside the back gate is the building which is thought to be St Luke's tomb. Even more intriguing is the legend that **St John** brought the aging **Virgin Mary** to Ephesus. Some 5km (3 miles) east of the ancient ruins lies the **Meryemana**, the house where Mary is said to have spent the last years of her life. In 1967, Pope Paul VI visited the site and gave it the official approval of the Catholic Church by declaring it authentic.

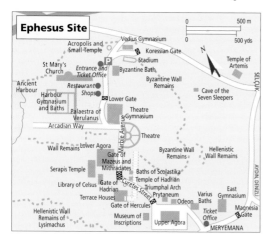

Selçuk **

Nearby Selçuk has a fine ancient citadel, which towers above the modern town. Here you can visit the **Basilica of St John**, a 6th-century Byzantine Church built on the site of **St John's tomb**, the precise location of which is indicated by a marble slab. This region was also the site of one of the Seven Wonders of the Ancient World. The magnificent **Temple of Artemis** (Diana) attracted pilgrims from all over the Near East. The site is today but a field of scrub halfway between Selçuk and Ephesus.

In the centre of town is the **Archaeological Museum**, containing some of the sexiest relics in Turkey. The likeness of **Priapus** (god of phallic fun) has long been a favourite with visitors. Less encouraging is the weird likeness of **Artemis** with her multiple globular attachments, first thought to be breasts, but now deemed to be testicles donated by her priests. Open 08:30–18:30 daily.

SOUTHERN AEGEAN COAST
Kuşadası *

Not long ago, Kuşadası was a sleepy fishing village, guarded by the tumbledown ruin of a **Genoese castle.** Now it is the liveliest **resort** on the Turkish Aegean coast and large **cruise liners** put in daily during the summer season. The coast around here is blessed with a number of superb **beaches**, many of which are now overlooked by large modern resort hotel complexes. The town itself is within easy reach of Ephesus and Selçuk, as well as

---

THE SEVEN SLEEPERS' CAVE

A few hundred metres east of the Ephesus site is a cave. It's said that during Roman times, seven early Christians hid here to avoid persecution and fell asleep while they waited. When they awoke, they returned to Ephesus, but noticed that everyone was wearing strange clothes. When they enquired about this latest fashion, they discovered that they had been asleep for 200 years.

COIN SELLERS

These are particularly prevalent at the approaches to Ephesus. A character will sidle up and show you surprisingly authentic-looking ancient coins. Few of these specimens *are* authentic, but you will face a long **jail sentence** if you try to take them out of the country. Most are clever fakes, stamped out from forgers' dies – but they are priced as if they were genuine. Either way, it's not worth it.

many other interesting sights further inland. It even has a few historic sites of its own. The old Genoese castle on the island of **Güvercin** has now been restored, and at night its floodlit battlements are reflected in the waters of the bay beyond the coloured lights of the cruise liners. Close by the harbour the ancient **Kervansaray** (once a hostelry for the caravans of travelling merchants) has now been tastefully transformed into a luxury hotel.

Just south of Kuşadası are some of the best and most popular **beaches** on the Aegean coast. Try Ladies' Beach or Tusan Beach, both of which offer all the usual water and beach sport facilities.

Priene *

This site lies 24km (15 miles) south of Kuşadası and is the most picturesque classical site in the region, even if it is of little historical significance. Priene stands on wooded hills above the sweeping valley of the Menderes River. There's a fine temple, an overgrown stadium and a high Acropolis with superb views.

Miletus (Milet) *

Another nearby ancient city is Miletus, birthplace of the first Ancient Greek philosopher, Thales. This was once one of the greatest trading centres in the entire Mediterranean, with distant colonies in Egypt and the south of France, until its harbour, too, silted up.

Below: *Sea, sun and sand at fabulous Altınkum beach.*

Didyma (Didim) **

Just south of Kuşadası lie the ruins of Didyma with its famous pillared temple, built by Alexander the Great. South of here is one of the finest beaches in the region – **Altınkum Plaj** (Beach of the Golden Sands), which is ideal for holiday-makers travelling with children, as there is no surf and **swimming** is absolutely safe.

Left: *The unique pools of Pamukkale have been known for their curative properties since ancient times.*

The Pools Of Pamukkale ★★★

Some 150km (95 miles) east of Kuşadası, lies the sight which adorns many travel posters: pools of blinding white crystal spilling down the mountainside. They receive their water from the warm springs nearby, whose minerals have gradually become encrusted along the slopes, forming these spectacular, **terraced pools**. Further up the mountain you can bathe in the warm calcium-saturated waters of the original **sacred pool** of the spring, which is now, rather incongruously, housed inside the courtyard of a large motel. A short distance down the road you can visit the ruins of **Hierapolis**, the ancient spa which sprung up to cater for those who had travelled here to take the cure. Nearby is a large *necropolis* (cemetery), with some intriguing 2000-year-old tombs – which would seem to indicate that the cure wasn't always effective.

BODRUM

Roughly 150km (95 miles) south of Kuşadası lies the booming resort of Bodrum, whose name means 'dungeon'. In former times this was a place of exile for courtiers and ministers who had fallen foul of the Sultan in Istanbul.

Despite extensive development the town retains its charm, and whitewashed houses cluster on the hillside above an ancient harbour with its **Crusader castle**. The modern town stands on the site of the ancient Greek city

---

AN ANCIENT RIVALRY

Greeks and Turks have never been on friendly terms. Recently this ancient rivalry came to a head once again, with a dispute over the ownership of various rocky islets off the Anatolian mainland. But there's more to the present conflict than time-honoured antagonism. The Aegean coastal shelf is thought to be rich in natural oil reserves. Each scrap of territory has its own territorial waters, which means that lonely uninhabited outcrops of rock – previously uninteresting – have now become potentially valuable.

of **Halicarnassos**, which was established as long ago as the 11th century BC. Several centuries later the Greek historian **Herodotus,** whose chronicles earned him the title 'Father of History', was born here.

From the waterfront at Bodrum you can take **boat trips** to the nearby islands and along the spectacularly beautiful coastline.

Above: *This romantic Crusaders' Castle lies at the entrance to Bodrum harbour.*

Castle of St Peter ★★★

This castle was started by the Crusaders in the early 15th century and completed in 1522. No sooner was it complete, than the Crusaders abandoned it, because Suleiman the Magnificent had captured their stronghold at Rhodes, so this outpost was no longer considered worth defending.

The structure remains largely intact and now contains some interesting exhibits of Mycenaean artefacts and Roman glass. It also houses the **Museum of Underwater Archaeology**, which features a superb range of booty salvaged from the numerous luckless vessels that have sunk in the Aegean off Bodrum over the centuries, littering the ocean floor with their cargo. Each hall in the castle is devoted to a different era – from the Mycenaean age onward. Open 08:00–12:00 and 14:00–16:00 Tuesday–Sunday.

The Mausoleum ★★

During the 4th century BC, Bodrum was ruled by **King Mausolus**, who built himself a tomb of such splendid magnificence that it became one of the Seven Wonders of the Ancient World. It was known as the **Mausoleum**, and is the origin of the word we use to describe a grandiose tomb. Nearly 2000 years later, the Crusaders used stones from the ruined

---

THE ERTEGÜN BROTHERS

Ahmet and Nesui Ertegün grew up in Bodrum. When their father became Turkish ambassador to the United States in the 1930s, the family moved to America. Here the brothers became so enraptured with American jazz that they set up their own record company: **Atlantic**. Within 30 years Atlantic had become one of the most influential labels in the business, featuring such stars as **Johnny Coltrane** and the **Modern Jazz Quartet**. Ahmet died several years ago and Nesui retired to Bodrum.

Mausoleum to build the castle which still guards the harbour. Nowadays, little remains of the Mausoleum but its foundations. Despite this, the site is worth a visit, if only for the small exhibition which fills in the historical detail and contains models of the original treasures removed by archaeologists. It lies a short walk inland from the harbour on **Turgutreis Caddesi**. Open 09:00–17:00 daily except on Mondays.

> ### APHRODITE
>
> **Aphrodite** was the ancient Greek name for **Venus**, whose name is much more recognizable to us as the goddess of love. The old Greek name is the origin of our word 'aphrodisiac', which means 'love potion'.

MUĞLA

Some 100km (65 miles) across the mountains lies Muğla, with some fine old wooden houses in its winding back streets. But the best thing to see here is the extensive **market** held every Thursday, one of the finest of its kind in provincial Turkey. Old women in traditional peasant dress come down from the mountains to sell peppers. Perfume and spice sellers set up their stalls, and there's all kind of local craftware for sale at excellent prices.

APHRODISIAS

About 150km (95 miles) inland from Muğla are the ruins of ancient Aphrodisias. In Roman times, this was one of the main centres for the worship of Aphrodite, goddess of love. Among the many fine ruins are the main **Temple of Aphrodite**, and a spectacular **Stadium** where athletic contests were held that rivalled the original Olympic

Below: *Aphrodisias' stadium was once a venue for glorious athletic games.*

Games. These ruins may not be quite as spectacular as those at Pergamum or Ephesus, but except at the height of the season, the crowds here are much smaller and you can take your time wandering about. The small **museum** contains superb ancient sculptures, including a chillingly lifelike portrait of an ancient prize-fighter. Open 08:00–17:30 daily.

The Aegean Coast at a Glance

The Aegean coast of Turkey can become very hot indeed in the summer months, with temperatures regularly around 30°C (80°F). In the winter it cools down somewhat, but is often rainy. By far the best times to visit this region are **spring** (March to the end of May), or **autumn** (September to mid-November). If you are planning to visit during the summer months, be sure to book early.

There are regular international flights to Izmir. Istanbul also has regular international flights, and from here you can fly on internal routes to Izmir or Dalaman. Direct international flights to Dalaman tend to peter out in winter. All the airports have car hire facilities, but you may also hire a vehicle at any main resort. While the Aegean Coast is turning into an increasingly sophisticated tourist region, it has also begun to attract unsavory elements and **drug smuggling** is on the increase. Don't accept drugs (the penalties are horrific) and never have anything to do with someone else's luggage, unless they are personally well known to you.

Pergamum
Buses between Izmir and Bergama (the town below the ruins) run almost every hour, as does the bus to Ayvalık. The journey takes around two hours. Make sure you board a direct bus, or you'll be dropped 7km (4.3 miles) outside of town. If this does happen, however, you'll usually be able to hitch a lift for the rest of the way.

Kuşadası
Direct buses from Izmir are available every hour and the journey takes less than two hours. Dolmuş services are even more frequent.

Ephesus
There are frequent dolmuş services between Kuşadası and Selçuk. They stop at the entrance road to Ephesus, from where it is a 10-minute walk to the site entrance. The entire journey takes around 30 minutes and you shouldn't have to wait longer than 20 minutes for a dolmuş back. If you take the dolmuş to Selçuk you can walk the 3km (2 miles) to Ephesus, which takes you past the remains of the Temple of Artemis.

Pamukkale and Aphrodisias
Unless you are on a tour bus, the only way to reach these sights from the coast is by getting to the town of Denizli, which has regular bus connections with the coastal resorts. From here you can travel on by dolmuş.

Bodrum
There are regular bus connections between Dalaman and Bodrum, the trip taking three to four hours. The trip from Izmir is of similar length, with buses every hour.

This region attracts large numbers of tourists during the summer season. Unfortunately, if you ring ahead to book your accommodation this doesn't always guarantee that the room *is* reserved for you. Regardless of accepting bookings, many hotels simply continue to operate on a first-come first-served basis. This strategy does not normally apply to block bookings for package holidays, but has been known to happen in the past. Best arrive in the early afternoon to confirm your room – or give yourself time to find another one.

Bergama (for Pergamum)
Mid-range
Hotel Efsane, Izmir Caddesi 86, tel: (541) 12936. Pleasant, modern hotel with pool; on the road leading into town from the main highway.

Budget
Park Oteli, 6 Park Otel Sokak, tel: (541) 11246. Right by the Archaeological Museum. Accommodation is at a premium during the season in Bergama, but this quiet small hotel often has a room.

The Aegean Coast at a Glance

Bodrum
MID-RANGE
Artemis Pansiyon,
117 Cumhuriyet Caddesi,
Kumbahçe Mahallesi,
tel: (6141) 2530. Modernized
old-style pension with friendly
staff who speak English.
Ayaz Hotel, Gümbet Bay,
tel: (6141) 1174. On the
beach, east of the harbour.

Izmir
MID-RANGE
Hotel Kilim, 1 Kazım Dirik
Caddesi, tel: (51) 14-5340.
Refurbished, with views over
the sea from upper floors.

Kuşadası
LUXURY
Club Kervansaray,
1 Atatürk Bulvari, tel: (636)
44115, fax: 44119.
Magnificently refurbished,
300-year-old caravaners' inn.

WHERE TO EAT

Bergama (for Pergamum)
Bergama Restaurant,
Hükümet Caddesi,
tel: (541) 11274.
Here you dine on the terrace
outside, overlooking the
main street close to the
Archaeological Museum.
Sultan Restaurant,
Istiklâl Meydanı, no booking.
A charming, small restaurant
located in a leafy square in
the older part of town.
The service is exceptionally
friendly and the kitchen
offers a good range of
local specialities.

Pamukkale
Pamukkale Motel,
Pamukkale, tel: (6218) 1024.
This motel encompasses the
sacred pool. Try a dip
before you eat.

Kuşadası
Alarga Restaurant,
50 Atatürk Bulvari.
No phone booking. Excellent
seafront fish restaurant.

SHOPPING

All resort towns have their
souvenir shops. Best buys
are in leatherware – especially
handbags, jackets and shoes.
Carpets and kilims are very
good buys too.

TOURS AND EXCURSIONS

Regular coach tours run
from the main resorts such
as Kuşadası and Bodrum to
Ephesus and **Pergamum** and
to a lesser extent Troy.
There are regular coach tours
from the coastal resorts to
Pamukkale and **Aphrodisias**
(often including both in the
same tour, as well as a stop at
Muğla market on Thursdays).
It's a long trip up into the
mountains, and the entire

journey will probably take from
early morning to early evening.
Along the waterfront in
Ayvalık and Bodrum you'll
find boats offering a wide
range of excursions to nearby
islands and remote beaches
along the spectacular coast.

USEFUL CONTACTS

**Ayvalık Tourist
Information**, Yat Limani
Kasısı, tel: (663) 12122.
Bodrum Tourist Police,
tel: (6141) 1009.
Egetur Travel,
2B Talat Paşa Bulvari, Izmir,
tel: (51) 21-7925.
Izmir Tourist Police,
tel: (256) 613-1344.
**Kuşadası Tourist
Information**, Iskele Meydanı,
tel: (636) 41103.
Osman Turism Ticaret
(tourist and ticket agency),
18A Inönü Bulvari, Kuşadası,
tel: (256) 614-1205.
Turizm Seyahat Acentesi
(tourist and ticket agency), 60
Atatürk Bulvari, Kuşadası, tel:
(256) 603-1420.
Turkish Airlines,
Büyük Efes Oteli alti, 1F
Gaziosmanpaşa Bulvari, Izmir,
tel: (232) 484-5220.

IZMIR	J	F	M	A	M	J	J	A	S	O	N	D
AVERAGE TEMP. °F	55	57	63	70	79	87	92	92	85	76	67	58
AVERAGE TEMP. °C	13	14	17	21	26	31	33	33	29	24	19	14
HOURS OF SUN DAILY	7	6	9	10	10	11	12	12	10	7	8	5
RAINFALL in	4	3	3	2	1	6	2	2	8	2	3	5
RAINFALL mm	112	84	76	43	33	15	50	50	206	53	84	122
DAYS OF RAINFALL	10	8	7	5	4	2	1	1	2	4	6	10

5
The Mediterranean Coast

The western stretch of Turkey's Mediterranean region contains the **Turquoise Coast**, an area of exceptional maritime beauty with many picturesque beaches and inlets. Best known of these is **Ölüdeniz**, with its spectacular lagoon. This coastline is popular with yachting enthusiasts, as many of the more remote beaches and coves can only be reached from the sea.

The main resorts (and yachting centres) on this western section of the coast are **Marmaris** and **Fethiye**. Both have a lively nightlife, but are within easy range of secluded beaches and islands. Further down the coast you come to the idyllic resort of **Kaş**, with the tiny Greek island of **Meis** (Kastellorizo) just offshore. East of here is the island of **Kekova**, where you can see the remains of a Roman city beneath the clear water.

Between Fethiye and the booming resort city of **Antalya** are dozens of classical sites. Most of these date from the 1st millennium BC, when this stretch of coast was colonized by the Ancient Greeks. Some of the sites are in exceptionally remote and beautiful settings, and many have excellently preserved theatres and temples.

East from Antalya the coast is less well developed, but much of it is almost equally picturesque. Mark Antony gave the seaside city of Alanya to Cleopatra as a present, and just outside Anamur is a romantic Crusader castle. At the eastern end of Turkey's Mediterranean coast you come to **Adana**. Here you're closer to Damascus than Europe, and the region begins to take on a distinctly Middle Eastern atmosphere.

DON'T MISS

*** Marmaris: picturesque resort and yachting centre, makes an ideal base for exploring the coast.
*** Kekova: island off the Turquoise Coast with submarine Roman ruins and nearby Crusader castle.
*** Ölüdeniz: a spectacularly beautiful lagoon with good swimming beaches.
** Fethiye: main resort on the Turquoise coast, with ancient ruins in the vicinity.
* Alanya: the city which Mark Antony gave to his lover Cleopatra.

Opposite: *Sailing boats like this one are ideal for exploring the lovely coast.*

Above: *Boats bask in the sunshine alongside the pleasant waterfront of Marmaris.*
Opposite: *Marmaris has all the attractions of a developed resort, including plenty of shopping.*

CLIMATE

The **summers** are long and **very hot** along this stretch of coast, with temperatures often rising above 30°C (86°F). Winter however, brings storms and much cooler weather. The best time to visit is **spring**, which sees warm **sunny** days and flowers blooming on the hillsides. **Autumn** also has long warm **sunny** days.

MARMARIS

South of Muğla along the Rt 400 you come to the popular resort of Marmaris, situated at the end of a long inlet from the sea.

The enchanting coastline around Marmaris is dotted with beautiful, remote inlets and small islands, many of which have ancient ruins to explore. This has made the town a popular **yachting centre** and it now sports the largest **marina** in Turkey. A variety of yachts can be chartered, but this is an expensive business, often involving a large deposit, and is therefore best organized with a yachting agent in your own country before you set out.

Marmaris is favoured with one of the finest natural harbours in the eastern Mediterranean. In the 16th century, Suleiman the Magnificent anchored the Turkish fleet here, but when he came ashore, he took an immediate dislike to the local castle and ordered: '*Mimar as!*' ('Hang the architect!'). The town is said to derive its name from that remark.

Modern Marmaris has a hectic nightlife, with many discos and some excellent restaurants along the front. You can also take day trips out to the nearby **Loryma Peninsula** and the island beaches.

Unfortunately, Marmaris is presently in severe danger of being overdeveloped, with concrete-slab hotels springing up almost at random. The nearby international airport at **Dalaman** has made the town its obvious target for package tours. But things quieten down a bit at either end of the season, when the weather is still pleasantly warm.

Datça **

West from Marmaris the road leads out along the mountainous but narrow Datça Peninsula. Along its southern shore you'll find the pleasant, small resort of Datça, which is becoming increasingly popular. **Boat trips** to the more remote beaches further along the peninsula are available.

The best of these is to the ancient site of **Knidos**, which lies at the very tip of the peninsula over 30km (18 miles) away. Knidos now lies in ruins, but 3000 years ago it was one of the richest cities in the eastern Mediterranean. Travellers came from far and wide to marvel at the spectacularly lifelike, naked statue of the goddess Aphrodite (the Roman Venus). Others came to consult the physicians who practised at the celebrated medical centre here. Much of the present site is still being excavated, but the remains of the theatre can clearly be seen.

TRIPS TO RHODES

During the summer, regular ferries run from Fethiye to the Greek island of Rhodes, only 50km (30 miles) across the Aegean, a pleasant day cruise. At the other end you are at leisure to explore the town of Rhodes, which has a lovely harbour and picturesque Old Town. This was the medieval stronghold of the Knights of St John. You can still visit the cobbled streets and quaint inns frequented by the knights before setting off on their crusades to Jerusalem.

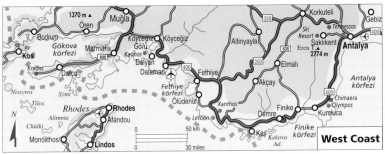

Dalyan ★★

This is a small, quiet town on the waterway between the
inland **Köyceğiz Lake** and the sea. The interesting ruins
at nearby Kaunos can be reached by boat from Dalyan.
Kaunos can also be reached by boat trip from the less
touristy Köyceğiz, which stands by its own inland lake.
On this trip you'll be able to see some fine examples of
rock tombs, which are over 1500 years old. Kaunos was
founded in the 9th century BC, and among the present
ruins there are a fine temple, a theatre, an acropolis and
a massive Roman bath, all dating from classical times.

From Dalyan you can take a boat downstream to
famous **Turtle Beach** (*Istuzu*), which is the breeding
ground of the rare **Loggerhead Turtles**. During **June** they
arrive by night to bury their eggs in the soft sand. These
hatch two months later, and the young turtles scramble
toward the safety of the open sea. Unscrupulous development of this area – which would have spelt certain death
to the turtles – was halted by a vigorous campaign led by
British naturalist David Bellamy. During nesting time, the
beach is closed nightly from 22:00–08:00 to avoid disturb-
ing the turtles, though there are conducted tours.

Upriver from Köyceğiz are thermal baths that are a
must for all men worried about their testosterone count.
These waters are claimed to increase male potency.

Below: *A boat ride to the
ancient ruins of Kaunos will
take you past fine examples
of Lycian rock tombs.*

Left: *One of Turkey's most photogenic spots, Ölüdeniz can be reached by a precipitous mountain road.*

TURQUOISE COAST
Fethiye ★★★

The town itself is rather ordinary, but its setting is a delight. Carved into the looming cliff behind the town are some rock tombs, dating from the classical era. The finest of these is **Amyntas' Tomb**, with its carved columns. Just west lie the ruins of a Crusader Castle.

Ölüdeniz ★★★

An exquisitely beautiful lagoon which lies just 8km (5 miles) south of Fethiye over the mountains, Ölüdeniz means 'dead sea', a reference to the fact that it is always calm, even during the worst storms.

During the summer this spot can become crowded, and is a popular anchorage for yachts. But it is definitely worth a visit for its beauty alone. Out of season it is a tranquil gem.

Xanthos ★

About 64km (40 miles) south of Fethiye, Xanthos was once the greatest city of Lycia. Largely owing to this eminence, it was repeatedly pillaged over the centuries, but much that was too heavy to remove still remains. This includes the famous **Xanthian Obelisk**, whose Lycian inscription has yet to be deciphered, an **acropolis** dating from Roman times, and walls which afford a superb view at sunset. The site is not enclosed.

YACHT HIRE

Much of the spectacular coastal scenery around Marmaris can only be reached by boat. On account of this, Marmaris has now become a centre for the hiring of yachts. It can be an expensive business, but prices become more reasonable if you hire out of season and make up a party. Hire can be arranged on the spot (a hefty deposit is required, as well as one person, at least, with a certificate of nautical competence). However, to avoid disappointment and other hassles, it's far better to organize before you set out. (For details of hirers, who often have international agents, see the small ads in travel sections of large Sunday newspapers, or enquire at travel agents.)

Above: Kaş harbour is one of the jewels of the Mediterranean coast.

Letoön ★★

Down the road from Xanthos are the ruins of the religious sanctuary of Letoön, which in classical times was a **shrine** of the **goddess Leto**. The site offers standing columns, remnants of mosaics of three temples, a theatre, and an ancient pool which is now home to local frogs and terrapins. Open 08:30–18:00 daily.

Olympos ★

This site lies 32km (20 miles) east of **Finike**. The origins of this picturesque seaside spot are lost in time. The main ruins lie scattered amid trees on the banks of a stream.

You can climb high above Olympos to see the eternal flame of the **Chimaera**, which is formed by continually self-igniting gas escaping from the hillside.

Kaş ★★

In the early 1980s Kaş was still a sleepy fishing village. Nowadays, tourism has arrived, yet the town remains largely unspoilt. This may not last much longer though, as Kaş is crammed between high cliffs and sea, and thus has nowhere to expand.

Standing by the road in the middle of town there's a **Lycian Sarcophagus** which is over 2000 years old, and to the north there's a fine ancient **Greek amphitheatre**.

Kekova ★★★

This island, whose large bay provides a popular anchoring spot for yachts, lies some 20km (12½ miles) east of Kaş. Offshore from Kekova the **submerged ruins** of a Roman city are visible below the surface. In a small bay on the island itself are the ruins of a Byzantine church. On the mainland, east along the bay, are striking rock tombs dating from the 4th century BC, and at **Simena** the ruins of a Crusaders castle. All these sights lie somewhat off the beaten track, but are well worth exploring.

ST NICHOLAS OF DEMRE

St Nicholas, the original **Santa Claus**, may have been the 4th-century Bishop of Myra. This town is now but a ruin outside Demre, a seaside resort 50km (30 miles) east of Kaş.

A TERRITORIAL FREAK

The small island offshore from Kaş is known to the Turks as Meis, but belongs to the Greeks, who call it Kastellorizo. It's only a few kilometres from the Anatolian mainland, but at least 100km (65 miles) from the nearest Greek territory, making it the most remote of all the Greek islands. During the summer season it can be reached by boat trips from Kaş.

ANTALYA

Roughly 180km (110 miles) to the northeast along Rt 400, you come to the port city of **Antalya**, which is superbly situated on a wide bay, framed by high mountains to the west. The city looks down over a harbour, which has a **Roman lighthouse** on the hillside at its southeastern approach. The citizens of old Antalya were so renowned for their fighting qualities that they remained unconquered throughout most of the classical era. Even Alexander the Great decided against attacking them, and the Romans thought it best to adopt a diplomatic approach, welcoming them as 'allies'.

Kaleiái *

Around the harbour lies the well-preserved **Old Quarter** with steep lanes, narrow winding streets and scattered Roman ruins. The main sight in Antalya is the famous **Yivli Minare** (Fluted Minaret), which is decorated with turquoise and dark blue tiles and dominates the slope above the harbour.

The Archaeological Museum *

To the west of town lies a good museum, where you can see many interesting classical relics that have been unearthed in the vicinity. Also on view at the museum is the urn which is said to contain the remains of **St Nicholas of Demre**, the kindly 4th-century Bishop of Myra, better known to us as Santa Claus.

CHIMAERA

The Chimaera is situated 80km (50 miles) south of Antalya. This eternal flame burns on a mountainside some 250m (830ft) above the sea. Ignition is caused by methane gas seeping up from below the surface, but the flame takes its name from the legendary beast that plagued this neighbourhood 3000 years ago. Chimaera had a lion's head, the body of a goat and a serpent's tail. Today the name is used to describe any grotesque figment of the imagination.

Below: *The distinctive Yivli Minare rises above the houses of Antalya.*

East Coast

Below: *Turkish carpets
for sale in Side.*
Opposite: *Alanya's
old castle perches high
above the modern town.*

St Nicholas would often make anonymous gifts to poor
families and was famed for his generosity. He usually
came around at night and dropped coins through the
chimney. After St Nicholas died, his fame spread all over
Europe and he became the legendary source of
Christmas presents. He was also adopted as the patron
saint of Russia.

AROUND ANTALYA
Termessos **
Along the coast to the south of Antalya are a growing
number of good beach resorts. This region also has
a number of fine classical ruins. The best of these is
the 3000-year-old city of Termessos, which is spectacularly situated high in the mountains some 35km
(20 miles) northwest of Antalya.

Side *
About 56km (35 miles) east down the coastal road from
Antalya you come to Side and its ancient remains, which
have been the site of extensive **archaeological excavations**. These ruins date from the Hellenistic era, when
Side was a fortified port. Despite concerted efforts,
the town has (just) managed to withstand the ravages
of mass tourism, but you can still expect to encounter
sizeable crowds during high season. Besides the fine
entry gate and well-preserved walls of the ruins, there is

also an Agora, a theatre,
and the **Temple to Apollo**
which romantically overlooks
the sea (sunsets from here are
great). The site also contains
a museum whose lovely
showpiece is the ornately
carved **sarcophagus of Eotes**.
Open 08:30–12:00 and 13:00–
17:00 daily. The modern town
is now a popular, booming
resort, justly renowned for its
lovely, sandy **beaches**.

CILICIA

Alanya *

East from Antalya along Rt 400, after about 115km (72 miles) you reach Alanya. This town has three **beaches**, and has not yet been ravaged by tourism – though there are ominous signs of random development.

In 44BC the besotted Roman general **Mark Antony** gave this entire city to his beloved Cleopatra, and in the 13th century the old town of Anamur was captured by Sultan Alladin, who established his summer capital here.

Also of interest is the **Kızıl Kule** (Red Tower), which dominates the eastern approach to the Old City. This impressive 30m (100ft) construction was built in the early 13th century and remains largely intact. Just 10 minutes' walk north is a subterranean cavern aptly known as **Damlataş** (Cave of Dripping Stones), which has some good stalactites. Open 10:00 until sunset.

Anamur **

Anamur lies 60km (37 miles) southeast of Alanya and is Turkey's southernmost point. West of the town lie the ruins of ancient Anemurium thought to have been founded by the Phoenicians. During the Roman era it became one of the most important cities in the eastern Mediterranean. Eight kilometres (five miles) east of Anamur is **Mamure Kalesi**, one of the most romantic and best preserved Crusader castles in the entire Mediterranean. Open 09:00–17:00 daily.

FERRIES TO CYPRUS

From the western end of Turkey's Mediterranean coast it is possible to catch ferries across to Cyprus. This island is at present divided, and the ferries from Turkey only put in on the northern side. It is **not** possible to cross from the Turkish sector into the Greek sector which occupies the southern part of the island. Also, Greece will refuse entry to anyone whose passport bears a TRNC stamp. Regular ferries leave from **Tasuçu** 80km (50 miles) east of Anamur, and from **Mersin** 60km (37 miles) southwest of Adana. There is also a hydrofoil service.

Adana *

This, the fourth largest city in Turkey, is mentioned in the Bible (King Solomon bought horses from here). **St Paul** came from Tarsus just 40km (25 miles) to the west.

The **Archaeological Museum** houses interesting exhibits, including some Hittite seals dating from the 15th century BC.

The Mediterranean Coast at a Glance

The summers along this stretch of coastline can be unpleasantly hot, with temperatures regularly above 30°C (86°F), especially further east. Winter means frequent storms, with temperatures dropping to around 7°C (45°F). The best times to visit are in the **spring** or **autumn**, when there are usually long, warm, **sunny** days.

There are regular international flights to Adana, Antalya and Dalaman, as well as internal flights to these airports from the main international airports located at Ankara, Istanbul and Izmir.

Regular air-conditioned buses and dolmuş services connect all the main towns and resorts along Turkey's Mediterranean coast, which also have car hire facilities. **Yachts** can be chartered at Fethiye and Marmaris. Most resorts have boat trips to nearby stretches of the coast.

Marmaris
LUXURY
Hotel Elegance,
130 Uzunyali Caddesi,
tel: (612) 12369.
Smart, modern resort on the edge of town, with facilities including two pools. Not too expensive for what you get.

MID-RANGE
Hotel Lidya,
130 Siteler Caddesi, Uzunyali,
tel: (612) 12940.
Large hotel with all mod cons and many facilities, including its own private beach. Friendly staff mostly speak English. At night there's a casino and extremely popular disco.
Otel Marmaris,
Atatürk Caddesi 54,
tel: (612) 11308.
Balconied rooms with fine views out over the town.

Fethiye
LUXURY
Robinson Club Likya,
Ölüdeniz Kıdırak Meydanı,
tel: (6156) 6010. Classy spot, 15km (9 miles) along the coast at Ölüdeniz (the famous lagoon). It has its own beach, and is run as a modern resort, complete with extensive facilities.

MID-RANGE
Otel Dedeoglu,
Iskele Meydanı, tel: (252) 611-4010. Pleasant, friendly hotel down by the waterfront. Rooms with good views, friendly staff.

Kaş
MID-RANGE
Hotel Mimosa,
Elmalı Caddesi, tel: (3226) 1272. Pleasant tourist hotel on the main street leading down to the harbour. Rooms with balcony views of the sea.

Kaş Hosteli,
Hastan Caddesi 15,
tel: (3226) 836-1271. Friendly tourist motel by the sea.

Antalya
LUXURY
Sheraton Voyager Antalya,
100 Yil Bulvari,
tel: (31) 48-2182.
This monster of a hotel dominates the western approaches to the city. It has over 400 rooms, many with superb views of the mountains and the sea. Prices are up to international standards, but then so are the facilities, which include two pools.

MID-RANGE
Hotel Bilgehan,
194 Kazım Özalp Caddesi,
tel: (31) 11-5184.
Large hotel in the heart of town, with air conditioning and English spoken by almost all staff.
Hotel Kişlahan, Kazim özalp Caddesi 194, tel: (31) 11-5184. Close to the bazaar and only a short walk from the Old Town and the harbour. Modern with medium prices.

Marmaris
Birtat Restaurant,
Barbaros Caddesi, Yat Limanı, tel: (612) 11076. Excellent seafood on the romantic waterfront by the yacht harbour. This is one of the top spots in town, but not excessively expensive.

The Mediterranean Coast at a Glance

Greenhouse Restaurant,
Hacı Mustafa Sokak,
tel: (612) 15071.
American and Mexican food
in a pleasant courtyard.
Ayyildız Lokantasi,
Eski Çarşi Sokak 26/A,
tel: (612) 12158.
Excellent local dishes.

Fethiye
Yat, Yat Limani Carsisi,
tel: (252) 611-3939.
Justly renowned for its
really excellent seafood.
Tahirağa Lokantasi,12 Çarşi
Caddesi, tel: (615) 16308.
Wide range of local dishes at
inexpensive prices.

Kaş
Eriş, in the main square,
tel: (3226) 1057.
An appetizing range of local
and seafood dishes.
Mercan, Hükünet Caddesi,
tel: (3226) 1209.
Close to the sea on the
eastern side of the harbour.

Antalya
Hisar, Cumhuriyet Meydanı,
tel: (31) 11-5281. Built into
the walls of the old fortress,
overlooking the harbour.
Excellent Turkish cuisine.
Restaurant Ahtapot,
Yat Limani, Kaleiçi,
tel: (31) 11-0900.
Atmospheric spot down by
the old harbour, with fine
shady terrace. Their seafood
is fresh and they have a wide
range of imaginative dishes.
Be sure to try the octopus.

SHOPPING

The best buys in the resorts
are leatherware (especially
shoes and handbags), as are
carpets and kilims. Little wall
hangers filled with various
spices make an aromatic and
inexpensive gift.
**Beware of buying ancient
coins**. If they are fakes, then
you've been had. If they're
originals, you're breaking
the law and could serve a
jail sentence if caught.

TOURS AND EXCURSIONS

Most resort hotels run their
own **organized tours** to the
classical sites. In general
these are informative and
reliable. The main boat and
yacht chartering centres
are Marmaris and Fethiye.
If you're planning to hire a
craft, you are strongly advised
to do so through an agency
in your own country. In this
way you will have everything
organized upon your arrival,
and will be able to pay the
hefty deposit in your own
country and currency. One of
the best charterers in Turkey
is **Yeşil Marmaris** (see details
under Useful Contacts).

SPORTS

This coast is ideal for a wide
range of watersports, especially at the western end and
along the Turquoise Coast,
where the most popular
beaches have facilities for
windsurfing, **paragliding**,
and **waterskiing**.
Snorkelling and **diving**
expeditions can be arranged
from the main resorts such
as Fethiye and Marmaris.
Marmaris is also highly
popular for hiring yachts.

USEFUL CONTACTS

Turkish Airlines
(Türk Hava Yollari)**:**
• Dalaman Airport, Dalaman,
tel: (6119) 1499.
• Antalya Airport, Antalya,
tel: (31) 42-6272,
**Antalya Tourist
Information Office**,
Cumhuriyet Caddesi 91,
Antalya, tel: (31) 11-1747.
**Marmaris Tourist
Information Office**,
Iskele Meydanı, Marmaris,
tel: (612) 1-2035.
Yeşil Marmaris,
Barbaros Caddesi 11,
Marmaris, tel: (612) 1-1033,
for the chartering of boats.

ANTALYA	J	F	M	A	M	J	J	A	S	O	N	D
AVERAGE TEMP. °F	55	60	60	67	76	80	91	94	90	76	70	56
AVERAGE TEMP. °C	13	15	15	19	24	27	33	34	32	24	22	14
HOURS OF SUN DAILY	7	8	7	10	11	12	12	14	12	8	7	6
RAINFALL in	4	3	3	2	1	1	1	1	1	2	3	4
RAINFALL mm	94	81	72	45	21	10	3	4	18	50	82	110
DAYS OF RAINFALL	10	8	7	6	4	2	1	1	2	3	7	11

6
The Heart of Anatolia

Paradoxically, the most prominent feature of the ancient centre of Anatolia is modern **Ankara**, which was chosen as the country's capital by Atatürk in the 1920s. Atatürk was determined to leave behind the Turkey of the Ottoman Empire and turn the country into an up-to-date secular society.

Ankara may appear somewhat soulless and cold in its modernity, yet it treasures its history and the **Museum of Anatolian Civilizations** contains the greatest collection of Hittite relics in the world.

At the major **Hittite sites,** east of Ankara, you can see the impressive 3000-year-old ruins of an enigmatic civilization, the cities and holy places of an empire which dared to challenge the ancient Egyptians in battle, in the very first 'world war', over 1000 years before the birth of Christ.

Further south lies the haunting region of **Cappadocia**. This area, with its curious natural pillars of stone and its cave dwellings and extensive underground cities which once hid thousands of inhabitants, is one of the most eerie spots on earth.

The capital of Cappadocia is the traditional city of **Kayseri**, which boasts one of the largest ancient bazaars in the country, as well as a 700-year-old mosque. Directly south of Ankara lies the Muslim holy city of **Konya**, once the home of the famous Order of **Whirling Dervishes**. This fascinating ritual ceremony, whose every movement has deep spiritual significance, is performed every year in December.

Opposite: *Kayseri has one of the largest ancient bazaars in the country.*

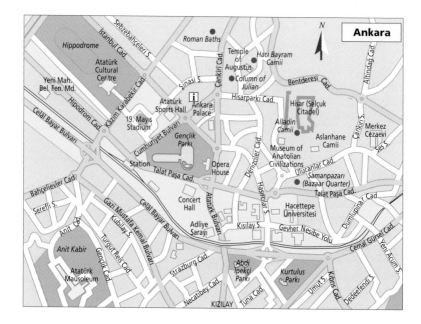

ANKARA

In Roman times, Ankara was little more than a small sheep-farming town. The sheep of Anatolia were famous for their **Angora** wool and the word 'Angora' is, in fact, simply a corruption of the town's name.

When Atatürk became president, after Turkey's defeat in World War I, he chose Ankara as his new capital. At the time it was a provincial backwater with a population of less than 30,000. It had no pavements, electricity, or covered sewers. Atatürk, determined to westernize, commissioned German architect Hermann Jansen, 'the man who built modern Berlin', to build him a new capital.

Modern Ankara lies in the heart of Anatolia some 425km (265 miles) east of Istanbul. It now has a population of over three million people, but at first sight is a rather uninspiring place. It has none of the exotic splendour of the former capital, Istanbul, but its citizens prefer it this way. For them, Ankara projects the modern, forward-looking face of Turkey.

CLIMATE

Summer in this region is not as hot as elsewhere in Turkey, and the lack of humidity makes it feel much **fresher** than on the coast. **Spring** and **autumn** too, are **cooler**, but winter can be severe, with midday temperatures remaining below zero.

The Old Town and Citadel **

A kilometre or so north of the modern town centre you can still see a few remains of Roman Ankara. Just east of **Çankir Caddesi** stands the **Column of Julian**, which was erected in the 4th century AD, to mark a visit by the Emperor Julian the Apostate. Northeast of here, the **Hacı Bayram Camii** (the city's main mosque) stands amid the ruins of the **Temple of Augustus**. Not much is left of this building, apart from the walls which date from the 2nd century BC, when they were erected by the King of Pergamum. Northwest of here, back across Çankir Caddesi, you can still distinguish the outline and ducts of the **Roman Baths**. Open 08:30–17:30 Tuesday–Sunday.

East of Roman Ankara, at the end of **Hisarparkı Caddesi**, you come to the **Selçuk Citadel** (Hisar), whose original walls were built by the Byzantines. Beyond the impressive gateway lie the twisting narrow streets and wooden houses of Ottoman Ankara. From the northern end of the Citadel, at Ak Kale, there's a fine view out over the city. The **Alladin Camii**, at the southern end of the Citadel, dates from the 12th-century Selçuk period. South of here you come to the **Bazaar quarter**, where Angora wool is still sold. In the midst of this district stands the oldest, biggest and most imposing Selçuk mosque, the 13th-century **Aslanhane Camii**. Inside there is an ornate wooden ceiling, supported by lines of wooden columns. The mosque is named after the Stone Lion in the court-yard (*Aslanhane* means 'lion house' in Turkish).

Museum of Anatolian Civilizations **

Some 300m (985ft) directly to the east of Aslanhane Camii is the Museum of Anatolian Civilizations. This is certainly the most interesting spot in Ankara, and houses the greatest collection of **Hittite antiquities** in the

> ### A ROMAN MISTAKE
>
> When the Ancient Romans occupied Ankara, they thought its name was the Greek word for anchor. The new coins they minted here proudly displayed an anchor on the back as an emblem for the city. Regrettably, Ankara is over 200km (125 miles) from the sea, which caused great mirth among its citizens. The Romans, who were not renowned for their sense of humour, failed to see the joke. Even when their mistake was pointed out to them, they refused to change the city's emblem.

Below: *Kite-flyers enjoy themselves on the topmost wall of the castle at Ankara.*

ANCIENT ANKARA

Contrary to its modern appearance, Ankara has been inhabited for centuries. The city was founded in the 7th century BC by the legendary **King Midas**, whose touch turned everything to gold. In early Christian times the city was part of the Roman province of **Galatia** and was visited by **St Paul**, who founded a church here. When St Paul continued on his travels, he wrote to the Christians he had left behind in Ankara. His letter appears in the Bible as the 'Epistle to the Galatians'.

world. The Hittite civilization flourished in Anatolia during the second millennium BC, and for a while their empire almost rivalled that of ancient Egypt. The fascinating relics and statues conjure up an intriguing picture of a civilization about which very little is known. Be sure to see the curiously evocative exhibit of the mother goddesses, some as old as 8000 years, which are thought to have acted as fertility symbols. Open 08:30–17:30 Tuesday–Sunday.

Atatürk Mausoleum **

Finally, no visit to Ankara would be complete without a visit to the Atatürk Mausoleum, erected in memory of the Father of the Turks. The suitably austere modernistic edifice, which nonetheless curiously echoes the Acropolis at Athens, is constantly guarded.

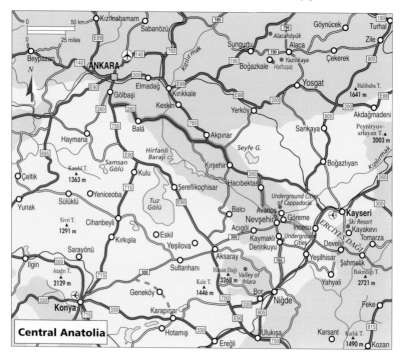

Central Anatolia

HITTITE SITES

References to the Hittites are made in both the Old Testament and in ancient Egyptian records. They arrived in Anatolia during the second millennium BC, yet, even today our knowledge of this great empire is still very sketchy. Unlike the Babylonians and the ancient Egyptians, Hittite civilization was not centred around the fertile

Above: *The Aslanlikapi, or Lion Gate, forms the main entrance to Hattuşaş, the Hittite capital.*

valley of a great river, but took the form of a highland existence. The Hittite Empire lasted for over 1000 years, and then vanished as mysteriously as it had begun.

Hattuşaş **

The main Hittite sites lie 120km (75 miles) east of Ankara. **Hattuşaş** was the capital of the Hittite Empire and even today its ruins cover a large area. A circuit of the site follows the 6km (4 miles) of city walls and will take you around two hours. The walk leads you to the **Great Temple**, the impressive **Lion Gate** (whose flanking lions are replicas, the originals having been removed to Ankara), the Sphinx and King's Gates, and the **Great Fortress** which was the residence of the kings and was approached by a ramp.

Other Hittite Sites *

About 3km (2 miles) east of Hattuşaş lies **Yazılıkaya**, the religious centre of the Hittite Empire, with its large ruined temple. Some 24km (15 miles) north of here is **Alacahöyük**, where there's a fine **Sphinx Gate**, a relief of a royal procession, and a secret tunnel whose purpose remains a mystery. The **royal tombs** here have been extensively excavated (all the finds are on display in Ankara). There's also a small **museum**, which contains a Hittite bath. Open 08:00–12:00 and 13:00–17:30 daily.

> #### CAPPADOCIA'S VOLCANIC PAST
>
> The entire region of Cappadocia is covered with outcrops of volcanic rock. These are all that remain of the massive lava flows from a nearby volcano which was active during prehistoric times. Nowadays, snow-capped **Mt Erciyes** is extinct, and its peak can be seen, rising to nearly 4000m (13,100ft) to the south of Cappadocia.

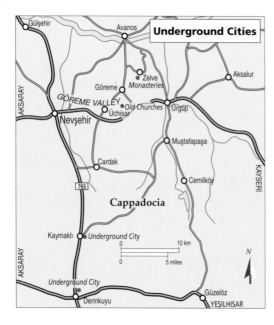

CAPPADOCIA

Cappadocia lies about 180km (110 miles) south-east of Ankara. This region of soft volcanic rock has been sculpted into pillars and columns of fantastic shapes by centuries of wind, snow, rain and erosion. The pliable rock was further changed by human hands, resulting in a stunning variety of **caves** and even entire **underground cities**.

The Hittites first lived in this area, but rock-carving began in earnest only after **Christian hermits**, most of whom were Greeks and Armenians, arrived in the 4th century. Cappadocia became one of the most import-ant early Christian centres in the eastern Mediterranean. Even after the area was conquered by Turkish Muslims in the 11th century, the local Christians were left largely undisturbed and continued living here until World War I.

Göreme ★★★

Göreme, the best site in the valley, has a superb open-air museum. Here you can explore several fascinating 1000-year-old churches. (A flashlight is worthwhile if you want to admire the remaining **frescoes** and **murals**, since the inside of most rock churches and dwellings is rather gloomy.) The most spectacular are the **Karanlık Kilise** (Dark Church), with its splendidly preserved frescoes of Christ and Judas, the **Elmalı Kilise** (Apple Church), and the **Tokali Kilise** (Buckle Church), largest of them all, which even features a small chapel downstairs. The nearby valleys, filled with weird rock formations, are honeycombed with eerie troglodite dwellings.

A few kilometres north of Göreme lies **Zelve**, with three valleys of abandoned, concealed **monasteries** carved into the rock, some of which date back to the 8th century, maybe even earlier. Eight kilometres (five miles) north of here you come to the pleasant riverside town of **Avanos**, which is famous for its **pottery**, some of which is displayed in cool underground caverns.

Derinkuyu ***

About 25km (15 miles) south of Göreme lies a truly spectacular, many-layered **underground city** (none of which is visible above the surface). Each tier is a labyrinth of tunnels, with living quarters for humans and animals, as well as wine cellars, bakeries and ventilation shafts. You may explore, but be warned – it's a claustrophobic experience.

Another intriguing underground city lies just north of Derinkuyu at **Kaymaklı**. This maze of tunnels and chambers is even more intricate and apparently haphazard. Be sure to follow the arrows which lead you through, otherwise it's almost impossible to find your way out.

> ### KING MIDAS
>
> In the 7th century BC Midas was the ruler of Phrygia, the kingdom traversed by the trade routes between Greece and the Middle East. During this era, Midas accumulated huge revenues from the caravans that passed through his territory, eventually becoming the richest ruler in Asia Minor, which led to the legend that everything he touched turned to gold. We still speak of 'the Midas touch'.

Valley of Ihlara **

Approximately 32km (20 miles) west of Derinkuyu lies the interesting Ihlara Valley, which was used as a retreat by Byzantine monks 1000 years ago. A number of their churches and chapels can still be seen, carved into the rocks or built out of local stone. Among the best are the **Church of the Snakes** and the **Church of the Hyacinths**.

This valley is dominated by the high cone of **Hasan Dağı**, an extinct volcano which still emits a plume of smoke from time to time.

Below: *The eerie rock dwellings of Cappadocia.*

Below: *In action, the Whirling Dervishes of Konya are a truly extraordinary sight.*

KAYSERI

Kayseri lies beneath snow-clad Mt Erciyes, an extinct volcano that is now being developed as a **skiing** centre.

Many curious **Selçuk tombs** are scattered throughout the city, the most ornate of which is the 13th-century **Döner Kümbet**, in the centre of a traffic circle close to the Archaeological Museum. The main mosque is the impressive 13th-century **Ulu Camii** (Great Mosque), which took over 100 years to complete. The **bazaar** quarter is an increasingly popular tourist destination. Particularly good buys are gold jewellery, carpets and kilims.

KONYA

Konya is home to the **Whirling Dervishes**, founded by the *sufi* (Muslim sage) Mevlâna in the 13th century. This holy place has been inhabited for almost 7000 years, and Hittite remains (now in Ankara) were found in **Alâeddin Park,** just west of the city centre. Here you can also see the 12th-century **Alâeddin Mosque**. Its odd shape was dictated by the building materials (stones and columns pinched from nearby Roman ruins).

Mevlâna Museum ***

The tombs of Mevlâna and many of his most illustrious followers is on view at the Mevlâna Museum. Besides being a museum, this is also a **shrine** and a destination of pilgrimage – so you must be appropriately dressed and remove your shoes before entering. Women's heads and bare arms must be covered and shorts are not allowed.

Karatay Medrese **

The **Karatay Museum,** 1km (½ mile) west of here, has superb ceramics and tiles. Don't miss the awe-inspiring **Dome of Stars** lined with beautiful Selçuk tiles. At its base is an inscription from the first chapter of the Koran.

The Heart of Anatolia at a Glance

Best Times to Visit

Ankara can be very hot during July and August, but it's not as humid here as it is on the coast. In winter it can become very cold, with midday temperatures remaining below freezing. The best time to visit is **early summer** or **early autumn**.

Getting There

Ankara airport has regular flights to all major destinations throughout the world. It also offers regular internal flights to all the main cities in Turkey.

Getting Around

There are internal flights between Ankara and Kayseri, which are also linked by rail. The main towns in this region are connected by regular bus and dolmuş services. The main sights are also serviced regularly by dolmuş, but less reliably so out of season.

Where to Stay

Ankara
Luxury
Büyük Ankara Oteli, Atatürk Bulvari 183, tel: (4) 125-6655. Smart, central hotel which is not too expensive. Also has a good pool.

Kayseri
Mid-range
Hotel Turan,
Turan Caddesi 8, tel: (35) 11-1968. Handy for all the main sights, and they also have a good rooftop restaurant.

Konya
Mid-range
Hotel Balikçilar, Mevlâna Karşısı 1, tel: (33) 11-2969. Three-star, modern hotel within easy reach of the sites and the bazaar.

Nevşehir
Mid-range
Hotel Orsan, Kayseri Caddesi 15, tel: (485) 11035. Pleasant, modern hotel. Most rooms have balconies, and there's also a good pool.

Where to Eat

Ankara
Washington Restaurant, Bayindir 22, tel: (312) 425-2219. Excellent Turkish cuisine and friendly service.

Kayseri
Iskender Kebap Salonu, 27 Mayıs Caddesi 5, tel: (351) 11-2769. Upstairs dining overlooking the busy streets. Good local specialities.

Konya
Şifa Lokantasi, Mevlâna Caddesi 30, tel: (332) 351-0519. As in most restaurants in Konya, no alcohol is served.

Tours and Excursions

Well organized tours to the **Cappadocia** area are available from Ankara through: **Setur Ankara**, Kavaklıdere Sokak 5B, tel: (4) 167-1165. Should you wish to join a tour to the **Hittite sites**, the best, also arranged from Ankara, is offered by **Konvoy Tur**, Atatürk Bulvari 233/8, Kavaklıdere, tel: (312) 425-4844.

Useful Contacts

Turkish Airlines
(*Türk Hava Yolari*)**:**
• Hippodrom Caddesi, Gar Yeni, Ankara, tel: (312) 312-4900.
• Gahabiya Mah, Yıldırım Caddesi 1, Kayseri, tel: (352) 233-1001.
Car rental agencies may be contacted at the following city outlets:
Avis, Tunus Caddesi 68/2, Kavaklıdere, Ankara, tel: (312) 425-2313.
Hertz, Kızılırmak Sokak 1, Ankara, tel: (312) 467-8400.
Ministry of Tourism, Gazi Mustafa Kemal Bulvari 33, Ankara, tel: (312) 230-1911.

ANKARA	J	F	M	A	M	J	J	A	S	O	N	D
AVERAGE TEMP. °F	34	30	51	63	73	78	86	87	78	69	57	40
AVERAGE TEMP. °C	1	-1	11	17	23	26	30	31	26	21	14	4
HOURS OF SUN DAILY	4	5	5	8	7	8	10	7	8	5	4	3
RAINFALL in	1	1	1	1	2	1	1	1	1	1	1	2
RAINFALL mm	33	31	33	33	48	25	13	10	18	23	31	48
DAYS OF RAINFALL	8	8	7	7	7	5	2	1	3	5	6	9

7
The Black Sea Coast

The Black Sea coast is one of the undiscovered pleasures of Turkey. The first surprise is how lush and green it is here. The mountains frequently rise steeply from the sea, making for some of the most breathtaking coastal scenery.

Jason and the Argonauts travelled along these shores in their quest for the Golden Fleece. This was also the home of the legendary Amazons (*see* p. 105), a fierce tribe of female warriors.

During the summer you can take the **ferry** from Istanbul, which calls at all the main ports along the coast as far east as Trabzon, which is just 160km (100 miles) from the border with Georgia. This is the easiest way to visit this region, although the rather long drive along the scenic coastal road does have its rewards in the form of deserted beaches and small villages.

Sinop is the oldest and most attractive of the coastal cities. Further east you come to **Samsun**, an industrial port and centre of the tobacco industry. Inland from here you can visit **Amasya**, a delightful small mountain town with many ancient mosques and a number of historic buildings. Travelling east from Samsun, you reach several small resorts, the best of which is **Ünye**. However, the most exotic destination in this region is undoubtedly **Trabzon**, which for a brief period was the far-flung capital of the Byzantine empire. Inland from here lies the spectacular **Sumela Monastery**. High in the mountains, this is the most distant, but also the most spectacular sight in the area.

BLACK SEA
SINOP
TRABZON
TURKEY
ADANA
SYRIA

DON'T MISS

*** **Sumela:** spectacular ancient monastery high in the mountains.
*** **Sinop:** historic city with a picturesque harbour, beaches and classical sites.
** **Trabzon:** romantic city made famous by Rose Macauley's book *The Towers of Trebizond*.
** **Ünye:** pleasant Black Sea resort.
** **Amasya:** historic, unspoilt inland town.

Opposite: *Tea plantations alternate with almond trees in blossom along the fertile Black Sea Coast.*

SINOP

Sinop, situated on an isthmus, is the most charming city on the Black Sea coast. It has a lovely harbour, beaches, classical sites and a lively summer nightlife.

The city is named after the Amazon **queen Sinope**, who managed to evade the designs of the lusty god Zeus by tricking him into granting her eternal virginity. Sinop was also the home of **Diogenes**, the famous Greek Cynic philosopher who rejected social standards and lived in a barrel. When Alexander the Great passed through here in the 4th century BC, he called on Diogenes, who was sun-bathing outside his barrel. Alexander was so impressed by Diogenes' carefree lifestyle that he offered the philo-sopher whatever he wished. Diogenes merely replied: 'Could you step out of the way, you're blocking the sun'.

There has been a fortress on this site since the 7th cen-tury BC. Most of the present **castle ruin** is around 500 years old. It was built by the Byzantines, with a few Selçuk Turkish additions. The city also has a **museum**, with several intriguing finds dating from the classical era. Most are from local archaeological sites which are still being excavated. Nearby you can see the remains of the **Temple of Serapis** (an Egyptian god, better known to us as Apollo), which dates from the Ancient Greek era.

To the west of Sinop the delightfully scenic coastal road passes through a long series of villages, with mostly empty beaches. The coastline here remains largely unspoilt and is only visited in summer, mainly by locals.

CLASSIC PARANOID

Sinop was the home of one of the most notorious kings of classical times. **Mithradates Eupator** was the paranoid ruler of the Pontic Empire, which covered most of north-western Anatolia in the 2nd century BC. He locked his mother in a dungeon, and then married his sister, by whom he had several sons. But evidently family life didn't agree with him, so he murdered them all. Later he decided to declare war on the Roman Empire and, after slaughtering 80,000 Roman citizens and driving the rest out of Anatolia, he thought he had won. But the Romans returned in even greater numbers. Mithradates Eupator was defeated, tried to poison himself and when this failed, ordered his bodyguard to run him through with his sword.

SAMSUN

This sprawling industrial city is the largest port on the Black Sea coast, and a centre of the **tobacco** industry. There's little here in the way of tourist attractions, but it has useful ferry connections to Istanbul and Trabzon during the summer.

It was at Samsun that Atatürk launched the **Turkish War of Independence** after the Greeks invaded at the end of World War I, an event that marked the inception of modern Turkey.

If you find yourself stuck here while waiting for a ferry, be sure to visit the local **museum**. The collection of relics reflects the city's long history, which began over 26 centuries ago. It's also worth walking around the busy port area, which has an atmospheric market where you can buy all kinds of Soviet mementos from itinerant Russian traders.

> **CLIMATE**
>
> The Black Sea coast is **temperate**, compared to the rest of the country. This means that summers are not too hot, with temperatures around 25°C (77°F). The only drawback is that it rains often, which can make this region seem a bit dismal during the colder seasons, even though the temperature doesn't fall below 10°C (50°F).

AMASYA

This historic mountain town lies approximately 125km (80 miles) south of Samsun in the picturesque valley of the Yeşil Irmak (Green River)and has remained largely unspoilt. The town itself has several fine mosques. The **Gümüslü Cami** (Silver Mosque) dates from the 13th century. Even older is the **Burmalı Minare Cami** (Mosque of the Twisted Minaret) – though the interesting twisting effect lies in the spiralling stonework, rather than in the structure itself. But perhaps the best thing about Amasya is its timeless provincial atmosphere. This is the Turkey very few visitors get to see. Walk around the streets and see the many ancient buildings which include such oddities as a 400-year-old Ottoman lunatic asylum.

Below: *Though heavily industrialized, Samsun retains some atmospheric old buildings.*

THE ORIGINAL CHERRY

The Romans first colonized this remote stretch of coast in the 1st century BC. They called the town we now know as Giresun, Cerasus. Here they discovered a luscious little fruit, growing on trees they had not seen before. This was the cherry, which had arrived on the Black Sea coast some centuries previously from China. The Romans soon began exporting *cerasus* to Europe, naming it after the town of its origin. Our word, cherry, is a corruption of the Roman name.

Below: *Tombs carved into the rockface above Amasya date back more than 2000 years.*

Tombs of the Pontic Kings ★

On the north bank of the river, a number of paths lead up the hillside to a cliff above the town, where several large tombs were carved into the rock, some over 2000 years ago. Nearby is the so-called Palace of the Maidens, where local pashas once kept their harems. Below the tombs is an old quarter of charming, wooden Ottoman houses. One of these, **Hazeranlar Konagi**, has been beautifully restored and now houses a small local **ethnology museum**. Open 09:00–12:00 and 13:30–17:00 daily.

The only way to the **citadel** is along the road leading northeast past **Büyük Ağa Medresesi**, a 15th-century seminary. Fine views from the top sweep over the town and the remains of the Pontic Fort.

ÜNYE

This pleasant little coastal town lies about 100km (65 miles) east of Samsun. Besides being a seaside resort it is also the 'hazelnut capital' of Turkey. The nuts are so plentiful around here that their shells are burned as fuel in winter.

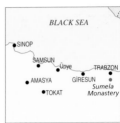

Left: *Many beaches along the Black Sea coast have barely been touched by tourism.*

The sea promenade is lined with shady trees and several modern hotels (though not as modern inside as their exterior might lead you to believe). Nearby there are several good **beaches**, the best lying to the west of the town.

Some 5 kilometres (3 miles) inland you can visit the ruins of a **medieval castle**, which affords excellent views out over the surrounding coastal countryside.

GIRESUN

This sleepy town lies just 130km (80 miles) west down the road from Ünye. The coastal ferry calls in here, and the main point of interest is **Giresun Adası**, an island 6km (4 miles) offshore. In prehistoric times this island was called Aretias, and was the home of the much-feared **Amazons**, a fierce tribe of female warriors. During the Byzantine era the monastery of St Phocas, whose ruins can still be seen, was established here.

According to tradition, the curiously pagan **Giresun-Aksu Festival** takes place around the island on 20 May each year. Locals encircle it with their boats, each throwing a pebble into the water and making a wish. This gesture is followed by wild celebrations.

Back in town, the most pleasant spot is the **Kalepark** around the castle, which is still surprisingly rural and is a good place for a picnic.

THE AMAZONS

According to legend, the Amazons, who crop up in several Greek myths, and are also mentioned in Homer's *Iliad*, arrived on the Black Sea coast in prehistoric times from India. They were a fierce tribe of warrior women, distinguished by the fact that they had only one breast. They are said to have cut off their right breast, because it got in the way of their bow-strings, and also impeded their javelin-throwing. The Amazons were a strictly female community. Once a year they would set out and round up a few promising males from nearby tribes. The hapless captives would then be forced to perform their duties, so that the Amazons could produce offspring. Only female offspring were allowed to remain members of the tribe.

TRABZON

For centuries, the former Trebizond was regarded throughout Europe as one of the most romantic cities of the East. It constituted the Black Sea end of the fabled Silk Route, which brought rare oriental goods and spices all the way across Asia from China. For a brief period during the 13th century, the city was even capital of the Byzantine Empire.

Today's Trabzon is a bustling commercial port squeezed between the mountains and the sea. It has several interesting sights dating from its moment of historical greatness. These include several ruined Byzantine churches, as well as the tumble-down remains of the palace which once ruled an empire.

The town itself has a lively **market** and interesting port area, both enlivened by **Russian**, **Ukrainian** and **Georgian** traders, willing to deal in anything. Until well into this century camel caravans would leave the Meydanı (city's main square) carrying pilgrims on the long trek across the Levant to Mecca. (These now travel by bus from the old camel stables.)

The Bazaar ★★

Ten minutes' walk east of the Meydanı you reach the bustling **Bazaar quarter**. Here you can buy anything from cheap ballpoint pens to live rabbits (for the pot, rather than as pets). More interesting for souvenirs is the port quarter, just northeast of the Meydanı, where you can find good, cheap leather jackets. This quarter has recently been colonized by tall, blonde Russian 'Natashas', whose fur-clad presence on the street corners is much appreciated by the local male population. However, they are also the focus of a female-led campaign which may rid Trabzon of all Russian commercial activity, even from the market by the port where you can

---

THE TRAPEZUNTINE EMPIRE

In 1204, after the sacking of Constantinople, Trebizond was briefly established as the capital of the Byzantine empire – which consequently became known as the Trapezuntine Empire. During this period, the name of the city became a byword for 'Byzantine intrigue', as its rulers sought to cling on to their crumbling realm. In order to appease the Mongol invaders from the east, they even sold off their daughters to Mongol chieftains. Trebizond's respectability was finally re-established by Rose Macauley's marvellous novel *The Towers of Trebizond*.

currently pick up all conceivable post-Soviet souvenirs – enabling you, for instance, to spend the winter after your visit, wrapped up in the cosy uniform of a KGB general.

Ortahisar *

A 10-minute walk up the hill southwest of the main Bazaar brings you to **Ortahisar** (Middle Castle), a district of winding streets and old houses occupying the old fortified Citadel. The **Ortahisar Camii**, just inside the northwest walls, is now the main mosque. The building dates from the 13th century, and was once the main Orthodox cathedral of the Trapezuntine Empire. At the southern end of the Ortahisar district are the ramshackle remains of the Byzantine Palace, from which the emperors ruled their ramshackle empire.

Aya Sofia *

Roughly 3 kilometres (2 miles) west of the Meydanı you come to the local Aya Sofia, which dates from the 13th century. This ruined building displays an odd blend of Selçuk and Byzantine influences. The showpieces here are the recently restored late-Byzantine **frescoes**, which somehow survived the Ottoman period when the building was used as an ammunition dump.

Atatürk's Villa **

About 5km (3 miles) west of town and reachable by regular bus and dolmuş service from the Meydanı lies Atatürk's villa. It was built at the turn of the century for a Greek banker, and is a rare example of the Crimean style. Atatürk stayed here several times, and the villa now houses an exhibition of his personal mementoes, including interesting old photos and annotated maps of his campaigns. Open 08:30–17:30 daily.

> ### SPIRITUAL ACCLIMATIZATION
>
> A good tip for acclimatizing spiritually is to read a translation of the Koran which you will find informative in many unexpected ways, as well as being enlightening and providing a good read. However, do not initiate conversations on this or any other religious matters, even if a local broaches the subject. Be wary, tactful and sympathetic at all times. Such subjects as Sadam Hussein, for example, should be avoided at all costs.

Opposite: *Atatürk's villa outside Trabzon is now an interesting museum.*

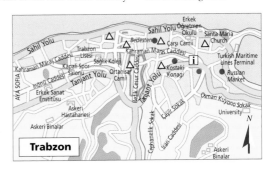

Below: *Sumela monastery, perched perilously above a steep gorge, contains many stunning frescoes.*

SUMELA

Some 50km (30 miles) south of Trabzon, high in the mountains amid the fir trees and mist above a steep gorge, lies the spectacular monastery of Sumela. According to legend, it was founded in the 4th century by a Greek monk called Barabas, who had been led to this remote spot by a sacred icon of the Virgin. The image, said to have been painted by St Luke, was renowned for its miraculous powers.

For many centuries this monastery was one of the holy centres of the Byzantine Church, and was even visited by Ottoman sultans as a mark of respect. It flourished until the early years of the 20th century, when its monks were shipped back to Greece after the Greco–Turkish conflict that followed World War I. The ruined monastery and superb frescoes are at present undergoing restoration, but the site is open to the public. It is reached by way of a 40-minute walk up a steep mountain track, which affords spectacular views across the gorge and down the wooded valley.

While you walk up, you see the monastery clinging to the sheer rock face high above you. There is something almost Tibetan in its remote fastness and inaccessibility, curiously echoed by its cliff-hanging external architecture beneath the rock face and the circling eagles above.

The Black Sea Coast at a Glance

BEST TIMES TO VISIT

Summer is the best time to visit the Black Sea coast. Even in summer it can be fairly wet, but at other times it's cool as well and the roads are prone to flooding. Also, the ferry from Istanbul, which calls at all the main towns along the coast, only runs between mid-April and mid-October.

GETTING THERE

There are internal flights from Istanbul and Ankara to Sinop, Samsun and Trabzon. **Turkish Maritime Lines** operate a ferry service from Istanbul, which runs all the way along the coast as far as Trabzon. There are also regular buses from Istanbul and Ankara. But be warned: it's a long trip (eg: 12 hours from Istanbul to Samsun).

GETTING AROUND

The best way to see this coast is to catch the **Istanbul ferry**, which runs between Sinop, Samsun, Giresun and Trabzon (see Tours and Excursions). Otherwise, there are regular **buses** between all the main towns along the coast. You can hire a car in Samsun, Sinop or Trabzon.

WHERE TO STAY

Amasya
MID-RANGE
Turban Amasya Oteli, Emniyet Caddesi 20, tel: (3781) 4054. Several rooms overlook the river.

Samsun
MID-RANGE
Hotel Yafeya, Cumhuriyet Meydanı, tel: (361) 16565. Three-star tourist hotel on main square, with excellent, cool rooftop terrace.
Otel Vidinli, Kazim Paşa Caddesi, tel: (361) 16050. Old established hotel in the centre of town with pleasant rooftop restaurant.

Trabzon
MID-RANGE
Hotel Ozgur, Taksim Caddesi, tel: (031) 11319. Right in the centre of town, on the main square and close to the port.

WHERE TO EAT

Sinop
Saray Restoran, Iskele Caddesi 14, no booking. Popular with the locals (always a good sign), with an excellent range of seafood.

Trabzon
Meydan Kebap ve Yemek Lokantası, Taksim Meydanı, no booking. Renowned for its excellent kebabs; friendly spot overlooking main square.

TOURS AND EXCURSIONS

The Turkish Maritime Lines run a weekly ferry service (virtually a mini-cruise) that departs from Istanbul on a Monday evening arriving at Trabzon on the Wednesday morning. The ferry calls in at all the main ports. Be sure to book well ahead as this trip is very popular. **Turkish Maritime Lines**, Rihtim Caddesi 1, Karaköy, Istanbul, tel: (212) 244-0207. Both of the following travel agencies specialize in tours of the Black Sea region: **Kosmos Travel**, Istanbul, tel: (212) 241-5253. **Natolia Tours**, Istanbul, tel: (212) 255-2466.

USEFUL CONTACTS

Avis car hire agencies at:
• Lise Caddesi 24, Samsun, tel: (361) 33288.
• Hotel Usta, Taksim Meydanı, Trabzon, tel: (31) 23740.
Trabzon Tourist Information Office, Taksim Meydanı, tel: (031) 14659.
Samsum Tourist Information Office, 19 Mayıs Bulvarı 2, Kat 1, tel: (361) 10014.

SAMSUN	J	F	M	A	M	J	J	A	S	O	N	D
AVERAGE TEMP. °F	50	51	54	59	69	74	79	80	75	69	62	55
AVERAGE TEMP. °C	10	11	12	15	19	23	26	27	24	21	17	13
HOURS OF SUN DAILY	3	4	2	3	5	7	8	10	8	7	4	2
RAINFALL in	3	3	3	2	2	1	1	1	2	3	3	3
RAINFALL mm	74	66	69	58	46	38	38	33	61	81	89	86
DAYS OF RAINFALL	10	10	11	9	8	6	4	4	6	7	8	9

8
Eastern Turkey

The hinterland of Eastern Turkey covers a region almost as large as that occupied by the rest of the country. If you are planning to drive from Trabzon on the Black Sea to **Van**, and then back down to the **Hatay** on the Mediterranean coast, you should allow at least a week. Double this time span if you want to visit some of the more remote sites – such as the Armenian ghost city of **Ani**, legendary **Mount Ararat**, or the curious stone heads on the 2000m (6500ft) peak of **Nemrut Dağı**.

This exotic region feels very much like the Middle East. The holy city of **Şanlıurfa** is located only 50km (30 miles) from the Syrian border. Here, modestly veiled women walk through the streets, tribesmen in Kurdish headgear abound and Arabic is spoken.

This region was also the home of Abraham (Ibrahim), the holy man who is revered by the Judaic, Christian and Muslim religions alike.

The bustling streets of ancient **Diyarbakır** have changed very little over the centuries and you will encounter water sellers and traditional letter-writers still noisily plying their trades (even if the latter now use typewriters). For centuries Şanlıurfa and Diyarbakır traditionally looked to Damascus, Babylon and Baghdad for their trade.

Historically, Eastern Turkey has had a significant Armenian presence, and until World War I, Van remained a predominantly Armenian city within the Muslim heartland.

DON'T MISS

*** Nemrut Dağı: mysterious stone heads on a remote 2000m (6500ft) peak.
*** Mount Ararat: the snow-capped mountain where Noah's Ark landed after the Flood.
** Lake Van: an inland lake almost as large as Luxembourg, with a historic city on its shore.
** Ani: spectacular remote ruins of an 11th-century Armenian city, once rival to Baghdad.
** Antakya: the ancient biblical city of Antioch.

Opposite: *The Church of the Holy Cross lies on an island in Lake Van.*

Eastern Turkey

Erzurum *

Some 300km (190 miles) southeast of Trabzon lies the remote garrison town of Erzurum. It is the highest city in Turkey and you soon become aware of the thin, cool clarity of the air which can prove both bracing and enervating.

Erzurum's strategic position has ensured that it has been overrun by all the many powers who have passed through this region, such as the Armenians, Persians, Macedonians and Romans. In the 14th century it was overrun by the Mongols, and two centuries later it fell to the Ottoman Turks under Selim the Grim.

Despite its prevailing military atmosphere, Erzurum has several interesting sights. Just north of the city centre, the **Bazaar quarter** occupies the old city.

CLIMATE

The climate in Eastern Turkey varies considerably. The Van region is **very hot** in **summer**, and **fiercely cold** in **winter**. The southern cities and the Hatay are extremely hot in summer, but pleasantly warm for the rest of the year.

Just east of the city centre, at the end of Cumhuriyet Caddesi, you come to the **Çifte Minareli Medrese**, with its impressive façade and twin minarets (after which the building is named). To the west of the town centre is the **Halıcılık Enstitüsü** (Institute of Carpet Makers) which houses some fine examples of their art. As you walk around, you will notice several ruined tombs scattered about the city, some of which are almost 900 years old.

KARS

Continue 240km (150 miles) northeast from Erzurum and you arrive at the remote, windswept city of Kars, only some 50km (30 miles) from the Armenian border. In the 10th century this was the capital of **Armenia**, when the Armenian Empire was at its greatest, occupying the Caucasus and much of northeastern Anatolia. This was the city's golden age, though not much from this era remains. In quick succession it fell to the Georgians, the Mongols and Tamerlane of Samarkand and then, in the 16th centuryl, it was finally flattened by an earthquake.

During the 19th century it was taken by the Russians (you can still see some old Czarist buildings, as well as the **Russian Orthodox Church** which has now been turned into a gymnasium). Kars is the place where you must get your police pass to visit **Ani**, which is right on the border with Armenia.

Ani ***

The ruins at Ani are among the most interesting and remote in the country. There has been a settlement here since the Urartian era at the beginning of the first millennium BC. The city had its golden age during the Armenian occupation, which ended in the 11th century. During this period it is said to have had a population of over 100,000 and its splendours rivalled those of Baghdad.

Below: *The Yakutiye Medrese in Erzurum dates from 1310.*

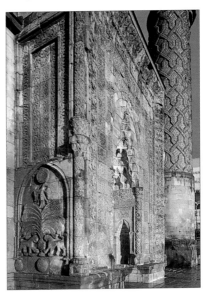

Above: *A boy herds goats across a landscape dominated by Mount Ararat.*
Opposite: *The citadel of the ancient city of Van was built atop a dramatic promontory.*

THE LOST ARK?

The biblical story of Noah's Ark landing on Mount Ararat after the Flood was usually accepted as a myth. Then in 1951, an expedition ascending the mountain came across several spars of ancient wood high up, preserved in the permanent ice. These looked curiously like the superstructure of a large boat. Photographs were taken of the exciting find, but subsequent expeditions have been unable to locate the exact spot where the wood was seen. It is thought to have been reburied by snowfalls. Increasing global warming, however, has renewed hopes that the intriguing discovery may once again reappear.

The ruins are entered through the **Alp Aslan Kapısı**, a Selçuk gate with a sculpture of a lion. Originally one of four gates, it is the only one still standing. Among the ruins are the remains of several churches. Best preserved is the **Church of St Gregory the Illuminator**, erected in 1215 by the Armenian nobleman, Tigran Honentz, and dedicated to the saint who converted Armenia to Christianity in the 4th century.

Some way below this church, on a ledge above the river, is the **Convent of the Virgin** (Kusanats). West of here you can see the ruins of the ancient bridge across the Ahuryan River (which now forms the border between Turkey and Armenia).

West from the Convent lies the **Cathedral**, which was started as early as 989 by Trdat Mendet and took over 20 years to complete. Nearby is the **Menüçehir Camii**, claimed to be the earliest Selçuk mosque in Turkey. It has a lovely mosaic ceiling, as well as a stub minaret which affords a good view of the ruins.

MOUNT ARARAT

Known in Turkish as Ağrı Dağı, this mountain lies at the easternmost extremity of Turkey, some 320km (200 miles) east of Erzurum. Its permanently snow-capped peak rises to over 5000m (16,400ft), and the mountain itself straddles the borders of Turkey, Iran and Armenia.

According to the Old Testament of the Bible, this is where **Noah's Ark** first made landfall after the Flood. The perfectly cone-shaped mountain forms a spectacular backdrop to the remote, flat plain, and nearby towards the Iranian border there is a large meteor crater.

For treks up Mount Ararat *see* At a Glance section p. 121. Application must be made at least three months beforehand. The last stages of the arduous climb usually require oxygen, and the hike is not recommended for inexperienced climbers.

Lake Van

This vast inland lake lies 320km (200 miles) southeast of Erzurum. As it has no outlet, the only loss of water occurs through evaporation, which has left the water saturated with such a **highly alkaline** concentration of mineral salts, that you can wash your clothes here without using soap. A word of warning: it's safe to swim in the lake, but the sodium will painfully sting any open wound.

Ahtamar Adası ★★★

This island in the southeast corner of Lake Van is reached by regular ferry from the mainland quay just opposite. It is the site of the **Church of the Holy Cross**, one of the most exquisite Armenian churches in existence. The detailed reliefs covering the outside walls of the church depict scenes from the Bible, including a doglike whale with ears, swallowing Jonah.

Van ★★★

This historic town lies on the eastern shore of Lake Van, about 100km (65 miles) from the Iranian border. The citadel of the ruined ancient city is on a promontory above the lake, known as the **Rock of Van**. This can be reached by regular dolmuş service from the town centre, 4km (2½ miles) to the east. The Hittites had a settlement here as early as the 13th century BC. On the north side of the rock is the tomb of a Muslim saint, which attracts pilgrims from far and wide. Above this is a rare and ancient Urartian temple, one of only a few discovered so far. At the top of the Citadel are the remains of an ancient castle and several mosques. Below the rock, to the south, you can see the silent ruins of Old Van, which was destroyed in 1915 during a struggle for an Armenian republic in Eastern Turkey.

VAN CATS

The Van region is home to the famous Van cats. These cats have distinctive white fur, and eyes of different colours. They are said to enjoy swimming in the waters of Lake Van, where they hunt for *darekh* (a rare form of carp), which has adapted to survive in the sodium-saturated waters. Legend has it that the Van cats originally arrived from India by way of the Silk Route. They may, in fact, have been brought to Anatolia by the first gypsies, who worked as metal-beaters repairing the shields and armour of invading armies.

The Van Museum north of the modern town centre has some fascinating Urartian gold ornaments, as well as figurines dating from this mysterious period. The upstairs section of the museum contains a display of skulls and bones related to the Armenian massacre of 1915.

THE SOUTH

Diyarbakır **

This is the ancient capital of upper **Mesopotamia**, which for centuries attracted Syrian, Persian, Babylonian and Kurdish traders. Some archaeologists believe that it may well be the oldest continuously inhabited city in the world. Remains dating back from as long ago as the Stone Age have been found on this site.

The ancient city centre is surrounded by walls that still have over 60 of their original 72 towers intact. The **Ulu Camii** (Great Mosque) is over 900 years old, and incorporates the remains of a 7th-century Christian church. The 16th-century **Safa Cami** is built in the distinctive Persian style, and near the east gate there is even an old **Surp Giragos Kilisesi** (Armenian Church).

Diyarbakır professes to be the 'World's Watermelon Capital' and each year at the end of September holds a festival to celebrate this claim to fame. The high point of the festival is the judging of the largest watermelon. Winning entries sometimes exceed a massive 50kg (110 pounds).

Below: *Locals admire the sacred pools at Şanlıurfa.*

Şanlıurfa

Travelling 180km (110 miles) southwest of Diyarbakır, you reach Şanlıurfa (Glorious Urfa), a city of biblical antiquity and religious importance.

Just south of the city centre lies **Abraham's Cave**, where, according to a legend sacred to Christians, Jews and Muslims, Abraham was born. It is said that Abraham sheltered here for the first 10 years of his life, evading **King Nimrod's** decree that all local children be put to death. Years later Abraham was captured by Nimrod, who ordered him to be burnt at the stake, but Jehovah made a spring gush from the ground which extinguished the fire. Nearby you can see the pools which are filled by this spring. The carp who live in it are said to be centuries old.

In the Citadel are the two ancient columns known as the **Throne of Nimrod**, and nearby is a Crusader castle whose ruins provide fine views over the city's old quarter. The bazaar is one of the most oriental in all Turkey.

Above: *Mysterious stone heads line the peak of Nemrut Dağı.*

Nemrut Dağı ★★★

This mountain of 2000m (6500ft) lies in the remote hinterland approximately 220km (140 miles) north of Şanlıurfa. At its peak you can marvel at one of the most amazing sights in Turkey: a collection of carved **stone heads.**

We owe this peculiar memorial to a human oddity called **King Antiochus**, who ruled a small empire in this region during the 1st century BC. Antiochus became convinced that he was descended from Darius, the famed Persian emperor, as well as Alexander the Great, and so decided to build himself a huge **tomb** with a temple complex at the top of Nemrut Dağı, as befitted a man of his station. This project had just been started when Antiochus' empire was overrun by the Romans. The temple was forgotten, and its remnants were rediscovered only in 1881 by the German engineer Karl Puchstein.

The famous stone heads are two metres high and represent the various gods which were worshipped in this region during the period. Each consisted of a melange of prehistoric, Ancient Greek and Persian equivalent deities, such as Helios–Apollo–Mythra. King Antiochus himself is

Above: *Once a city of fabulous wealth, Antakya retains a good deal of character.*

PILLAR SITTING

This early Christian craze was started in Antioch (modern Antakya) by **St Simeon Stylites** in the 4th century. This misanthropic anchorite spent a quarter of a century perched on his pillar, contemplating the evils of the world below. Occasionally he would deliver fiery sermons to the assembled populace. St Simeon soon attracted followers who also took to pillar sitting. At one time there were over 200 of these eccentrics occupying the moral high ground.

---

also represented, having assumed divine status prior to his demise. This touching 'family memorial' also includes the nearby **Eastern Temple**, which houses the beheaded statues of the gods, and a sacrifical altar which is now used as a landing spot by the helicopters that fly in our contemporary idols and semi-divine moguls. The combination of fallen divinities, clear, crisp air and sweeping views makes Mount Nimrod a heady experience you are unlikely to forget.

HATAY

This finger of land runs south along the coast and juts into **Syria**. The Hatay became part of Turkey as late as 1939, and many of its inhabitants still speak Arabic. Prior to 1939 this region had been ruled by the French, who used it as a secret diplomatic bargaining tool to keep Turkey out of World War II. A local referendum was held, and the inhabitants voted to become part of Turkey. The French handed over the Hatay, thereby ensuring Turkey's neutrality throughout the war. Doubts have since been cast upon the result of this plebiscite, which in turn have given rise to occasional unrest in Antakya, the main city of the Hatay.

Antakya ★★

Antakya (ancient **Antioch**), 320km (200 miles) southwest of Şanlıurfa, was founded in the 4th century BC by one of Alexander the Great's generals, **Seleucos Nicator**. Within two centuries Antioch had become one of the greatest cities in the world. It gained much of its wealth from being the main port at the Mediterranean end of the Silk Route, which brought caravans loaded with spices and rare goods from Asia. During Roman times Antioch, the third city of the Empire after Rome and Alexandria, gained a reputation for notoriously licentious behaviour, which attracted people from far and wide. Among these were a number of early Christians, determined to put a stop to all the debauchery (*see* fact panel at left).

Sen Piyer Kilisesi ★★

In a cave near Antioch **St Peter** founded one of the first Christian churches. Miraculously, this cave church, known as **Sen Piyer Kilisesi**, still exists. Here the apostle preached to his flock of early Christians, who worshipped in fear of their lives since Christianity was banned at the time. Mosaics on the floor date from AD500.

Antakya Archaeological Museum ★★

The other main sight in Antakya is the Archaeological Museum, which houses one of the world's best collections of **Roman mosaics**, preserved much as they must have been 2000 years ago. Some depict mythological scenes, others show scenes from everyday Roman life, giving us an insight into what the Ancient Romans must have been like as people. Open 09:00–12:00 and 13:30–18:00 daily.

Harbiye ★★

The **resort** of Harbiye can be reached by regular dolmuş from the city bus station. Since earliest times this has been a popular spot with locals fleeing the heat of the city. The attractions at Harbiye include a **waterfall** and a **cool leafy valley** with pools and tinkling water among the popular tea houses.

> **A ROMANTIC SPOT**
>
> According to legend, Harbiye is where the god Apollo fell in love with the nymph Daphne. He chased her along the river bank, but no sooner had he put his arms around her than she turned into a laurel tree. (Daphne means 'laurel' in Ancient Greek.) After this, whenever Apollo sang of his love for Daphne he decorated his lyre with laurel leaves and, in commemoration, a laurel crown was awarded to the winner at Ancient Greek music contests.

Left: *A mosaic of 'Orpheus Charming the Beasts' on display in Antakya's Archaeological Museum.*

Eastern Turkey at a Glance

Although the climate varies from region to region in Eastern Turkey, it invariably gets very hot during summer and it is therefore advisable to have frequent sips of water or juice in order to avoid **dehydration**. Also ensure that you ingest sufficient salt, since perspiration deprives the body of essential minerals. If not replenished, this could lead to a feeling of weakness, dizzy spells and even fainting. In winter, the mountain regions can become extremely cold. The very best times to visit this region are during **spring** or **autumn**.

There are regular internal flights from Istanbul and Ankara to all the main cities in this region. Erzurum and Van may also be reached by way of long and tortuous railway journeys from Ankara. Equally tortuous are the long and uncomfortable bus trips which link all the main cities to other parts of the country.

The only feasible way to get around in this region is by car, especially if you want to visit some of the more remote sights. The main roads are generally tarred and perfectly driveable in an ordinary saloon car.

The same applies to the road to Ani, although the road to Nemrut Dağı is merely a track in places. One of the best journeys in this region is by ferry from the town of Van to Tatvan which lies over 100km (65 miles) west across the oily-calm waters of Lake Van. You can then take the bus back around the southern shores of the lake, past Ahtamar Island.

Antakya
MID-RANGE
Büyük Antakya Oteli,
Atatürk Caddesi 8,
tel: (891) 35860.
A large hotel in the modern section of town, with a good air-conditioning system.
Atahan Oteli,
Hürriyet Caddesi 28,
tel: (891) 11036.
Useful 30-room, one-star accommodation situated close by the bazaar, with first-floor lobby.

Diyarbakır
MID-RANGE
Hotel Derya,
İnönü Caddesi 13,
tel: (831) 14966.
Small modernized hotel. There are several others nearby if this one is full.
Turistik Otel,
Ziya Gökalp Bulvari 7,
tel: (831) 47550.
Top-notch hotel with good range of amenities for far-eastern Turkey.

Erzurum
BUDGET
Oral Otel,
Terminal Caddesi 3,
tel: (011) 19740.
A modest but clean and friendly spot with some interesting travelling clientele.

Kars
BUDGET
Turistik Hotel Sarıkamış,
Halk Caddesi 64,
tel: (0229) 1176.
A very pleasant spot with somewhat spartan rooms that is situated west of town at Sarıkamış. Several new hotels are to be built in this area in the future.

Şanlıurfa
MID-RANGE
Hotel Harran,
Atatürk Bulvarı,
tel: (871) 34918.
Many travellers consider this to be the best hotel in town; good air conditioning.

Van
MID-RANGE
Büyük Urartu,
Hastane Caddesi 60,
tel: (61) 10660.
The best hotel in this town, with tasteful decor and very friendly service.
Hotel Akdamar,
Kazim Karabekir Caddesi 56,
tel: (61) 18100.
A three-star hotel located conveniently close to the Tourist Information Office. Also has a good friendly bar.

Eastern Turkey at a Glance

WHERE TO EAT

Antakya
The best restaurants tend to be found in the better hotels.
Oteli Atahan,
Hürriyet Caddesi 28,
tel: (316) 212-1407.
The menu includes good local and Middle Eastern dishes.
Saray Restaurant, Hürriyet Caddesi, Akbank Karsısı,
tel: (316) 214-7139.
A popular local spot with the usual no-frills decor and friendly service.

Diyarbakır
Once again, the best restaurants in town are usually found in the best hotels. The one in the **Turistik Oteli** (see Where to Stay) is quite good, as are the following:
Kent Lokantası, Kibris Caddesi 31/A, tel: (831) 10899.
The very best in town, it offers an excellent, mouthwatering range of tasty local dishes. Please note:
no alcohol is served here.
Hotel Demir, Ziya Gökalp Bulvari 7. Serves its meals on the roof.

Erzurum
Salon Çağin, Cumhuriyet Caddesi, tel: (442) 202-8741.
Smart by local standards. The service is friendly and a good range of regional dishes are on offer.
Salon Asya, Cumhuriyet Caddesi 21, tel: (442) 211-5763. One of the better local dining spots, regional fare.

Şanlıurfa
Here you're better off eating at one of the main hotels.
Hotel Harran (see Where to Stay). Definitely the best, and at the time of writing was still serving alcohol which is a rarity in Şanlıurfa.

Van
Here too, the best meals tend to be served in the smarter hotels like **Hotel Akdamar** and the **Büyük Urartu** (see Where To Stay). For more modest fare at a more reasonable price try:
Turistic Köşk Restoran, Cumhuriyet Caddesi. No bookings, standard fare with tasty regional variations. Very popular with the locals.

TOURS AND EXCURSIONS

Treks to climb **Mount Ararat** are organized by:
Trek Travel, Aydele Caddesi 10, Taksim, Istanbul, tel: (1) 155-1642.
Excursions to **Nemrut Dağı** are offered by several companies in Şanlıurfa. The most reliable of these is: **As Urfa**, opposite the Şanlıurfa Tourist Information Office on Asfalt

Caddesi, tel: (414) 211-1616.
Trips to **Ani** can be arranged by contacting the:
Tourist Information Office, Ali Bey Caddesi, Kars.

USEFUL CONTACTS

Antakya Tourist Information Office, Atatürk Caddesi 41, tel: (891) 12636.
Van Tourist Information Office, Cumhuriyet Caddesi 127, tel: (061) 12018.
Turkish Airlines, Hipodrom Caddesi, Gar Yanı, Ankara, tel: (4) 309-0400.

USEFUL WORDS AND PHRASES

Yes • *Evet*
No • *Hayir*
Thank you • *Teşekkür ederim*
I do not understand you • *Anlamadım*
Do you speak English? • *Ingilizce biliyormusunuz?*
Yesterday • *Dün*
Today • *Bugün*
Tomorrow • *Yarın*
Good • *Iyi*
Bad • *Kötü*
Foreign exchange • *Kambiyo*
Inexpensive • *Ucuz*
Expensive • *Pahalı*

KARS	J	F	M	A	M	J	J	A	S	O	N	D
AVERAGE TEMP. °F	21	25	34	50	63	70	77	79	71	59	44	29
AVERAGE TEMP. °C	-6	-4	1	10	17	21	25	26	22	15	7	-2
HOURS OF SUN DAILY	8	6	7	10	11	12	12	13	10	8	7	6
RAINFALL in	1	1	1	2	3	3	2	2	1	2	1	1
RAINFALL mm	28	28	28	43	86	74	53	53	31	41	31	25
DAYS OF RAINFALL	7	7	8	9	15	12	8	7	5	7	6	7

Travel Tips

Tourist Information
Ministry of Tourism,
Gazi Mustafa Kemal Bulvarı,
Ankara, tel: (312) 230-1911.
Main overseas offices:
UK: First Floor, 170/173
Piccadilly, London W1V 9DD,
tel: (0171) 734-8681,
fax: 491-0773.
USA: 821 United Nations
Plaza, New York NY 10017,
tel: (212) 687-2194,
fax: 599-7568.
Austria: Singerstrasse
2/VIII, 1010 Vienna,
tel: (222) 512-2128,
fax: 513-8326.
Netherlands:
Herengracht 451,
1017 BS Amsterdam,
tel: (20) 26-6810,
fax: 22-2283.
Sweden: Kungsgaten 3,
11143 Stockholm, tel: (8)
21-8620, fax: 723-1828.
Denmark: Vesterbrogade
11A, 1620 Copenhagen V,
tel: (1) 22-3100, fax: 22-9068.

Entry Requirements
Citizens of the UK and Ireland
need a **visa** to enter Turkey,
which is obtainable at the airport on entry. Citizens of all
other western European
countries, as well as the USA
and Canada, Hong Kong and
Jamaica only require **valid
passports**. Arrangements are
being made with several other
countries for visa-free entry,
but if in doubt, you should
enquire at your local Turkish
Embassy before departure.
For stays in excess of the
allotted 90-day period a
residence permit (*ikamet
tezkeresi*) is required, as well
as documented proof that you
are able to support yourself.
This permit is best applied for
at your local Turkish Embassy
well before you intend to
travel, as the paperwork
is long and complex.

Customs
Entry into Turkey is comparatively easy and painless from
a customs point of view.
There are a few nominal limits
on **duty-free** goods, mainly:
400 cigarettes or 50 cigars or
200g tobacco, 1.5kg of coffee
(including instant), and 5 litres
of spirits. You may be required
to list the serial numbers of
your photographic and video
equipment, as well as any
other electronic gear (such as
a personal computer).
These numbers will be entered
in your passport to ensure
that you don't sell them
while you're in the country.
Customs inspections on the
way out are much more
serious. Anyone who con-
templates taking out even
the smallest amount of
illegal substances should
take note of the word of
warning on p. 76. There is
no doubt that Turkish jails
are particularly punishing,
and long stays could ser-
iously damage your health.
The other main source of
interest to Turkish customs
officers is **antiques**. Ensure
that anything you buy, which
might possibly fall into this
class, is accompanied by a
purchase certificate from
the vendor, and that you are
indeed allowed to export
your acquisition. If in doubt,
contact the local Tourist
Police before you buy, and
make sure that they too
give you evidence supporting
their verdict on the matter.
Those found smuggling out
antiquities are likely to end
up in jail for long periods.

Health Requirements

No vaccination certificates are required for entry into Turkey. However, if you plan to visit remote areas, especially in the east, you are advised to have tetanus, typhoid and hepatitis jabs as a precaution.

Getting There

By Air: This is by far the easiest way to reach Turkey. **Ankara** and **Istanbul International Airports** have routine flights to and from most countries throughout the world. Regular international flights also arrive at Izmir and Dalaman. The latter tend to be links with western Europe. During the tourist season there are also a large number of charter flights to all these airports.

By Ferry: There are regular ferry services between Greece and Turkey, the main ones being those between Chios and Çesme, Samos and Kuşadası, Rhodes and Marmaris.

By Road: It is possible to travel overland from Bulgaria and Greece.

What to Pack

Turkey can be very hot indeed in summer, so be sure to take the coolest beach and casual wear. During spring and autumn it is still warm, but temperatures often drop in the evenings, so you'll need a cardigan or jacket. Winters are cool and wet on the coast, and you are advised to pack anoraks and sweaters. Inland and in the mountains it often becomes very cold in winter,

so be prepared to wrap up. Almost all restaurants accept casual wear, but some of the smarter ones draw the line at beachwear in the evenings. It's always worth packing some smart attire. If you go trekking, or plan to walk off the beaten track, be sure to bring some strong boots. Never set off for walks in the country in sandals and always ensure that your head is covered, as well as your arms and legs if possible, to avoid painful sunburn. Nude or topless bathing is not allowed in Turkey. There are, however, some very remote beaches . . . Be sure to dress modestly if you travel to villages away from the main tourist areas. Revealing beachwear here is liable to elicit offence. When visiting a mosque, you will be required to remove your shoes, women will have to cover their heads, arms and upper legs, and shorts are not permitted.

Money Matters

Currency: The Turkish lira (TL) has suffered from devaluation and massive inflation over the past few years, so expect to handle high-denomination currency. Coins are often worth more as scrap metal. Banknotes start at 5000TL, and escalate to 10,000TL, 20,000TL, 50,000TL, 100,000TL, 250,0000TL, and 500,000TL. Life is complex at this mega-mathematical level, so be sure to pay attention when settling bills.

Exchange: Banking hours are 08:30–noon, 13:30–17:00 Monday–Friday.

PUBLIC HOLIDAYS

1 January • New Year's Day
February (variable) • Ramadan and Şeker Bayrami
23 April • National Independence Day
19 May • Atatürk's Birthday
May • Kurban Bayrami (68 days after the end of Ramadan)
30 August • Victory Day
29 October • Republic Day
10 November • Anniversary of Atatürk's Death

In the resorts they sometimes stay open later in the evening. You can also change money at post offices, which are open 09:00–17:00, Monday–Friday. Better hotels will also change money for you, but keep an eye on the commission rates. Credit cards and traveller's cheques are not yet widely used in Turkey. Few restaurants and hotels accept them – especially away from the main tourist areas. However, they remain useful for car hire purposes, and for purchasing plane and ferry tickets.

Tipping: In most restaurants 10–15% is added to your bill. With taxis, it's customary to round up your fare. Beware: various attendants in tourist spots will optimistically try for a tip where none is required. The tipping of Turkish bath attendants is customary.

Accommodation

On the whole, accommodation in Turkey is inexpensive. The bottom end of the market can be very affordable, but is best avoided due to fleas and bed bugs. Each town will have at least one clean, reasonable **hotel**; all hotels are required by law to display their prices. Cities and resorts offer a wide range of hotels. Western-style smartness does not necessarily mean Western-style prices, but out of season, rates can often be bargained down a little.

Eating Out

Turkey has several different types of restaurant. Top of the list is the **restoran**. The best in Istanbul and Ankara are comparable to establishments found in any major metropolis. The ones which specialize in Ottoman cuisine (ie. food consumed by the sultans) provide a superb culinary experience amid smart decor. Lesser restorans such as those in the resorts will often have a fair range of international cuisine. Next is the **locanta**, cheap, cheerful and plentiful. Here you'll taste authentic local cuisine at very reasonable prices, often served in a cafeteria setting. The range of choice is much wider than you'd expect.

Lowest on the scale, but none the worse for that, is the **kebabci**. These invariably have a large *kebap* on a revolving skewer. Slices of *kebap* with salad and yoghurt, in a piece of pitta bread, can make a filling snack or an inexpensive meal. Another type of fast-food joint is the **pideci**, which serves the Turkish equivalent of pizza, baked in an oven.

Transport

Air: Turkey has a good network of internal flights, which link all the major provincial cities. The major hubs of this network are Istanbul and Ankara, which are linked by nine flights daily. Be sure to book well ahead and around public holidays.

Buses: Turkey has an excellent system of long distance air-conditioned buses which are run by a profusion of companies, and are often amazingly inexpensive.

Car Hire: Compared to other local prices, car hire in Turkey is very expensive. Indeed, you'll end up paying more than you would in most western European countries. All the leading international car hire firms have offices at the main international airports, cities and resorts. There are cheaper local companies, but they are not so reliable, and if you're planning to drive off the main routes, the one thing you will need is a sound vehicle. Turkey's main roads are usually up to standard, but things can deteriorate alarmingly if you wander off into the

wilderness. It's at times like these that reliability is an absolute requirement.

Road Rules: All distances and speed limits are marked in kilometres, with internationally recognized signs; signposting dwindles, along with the condition of the road surface, the further one travels away from the main centres. Outside of towns, roads are unlit and caution is advised.

Taxis: Most cities are jammed with taxis. Insist that the meter is turned on before you start your journey. Sometimes you may be asked to pay 10 times the price shown on the meter, because the meter is 'old'. However, it will not be as old as this feeble ruse. Most Turkish taxi drivers are honest and friendly. They are also required to have a large number on the side of their cab, which can be noted and reported to the Tourist Police if the driver fails to conform to the first of the above-mentioned virtues.

Dolmuş: This minibus service covers most of the shorter bus routes and inner cities. It's a bit more expensive than the bus, but more friendly and often

CONVERSION CHART		
FROM	**TO**	**MULTIPLY BY**
Millimetres	Inches	0.0394
Metres	Yards	1.0936
Metres	Feet	3.281
Kilometres	Miles	0.6214
Kilometres square	Square miles	0.386
Hectares	Acres	2.471
Litres	Pints	1.760
Kilograms	Pounds	2.205
Tonnes	Tons	0.984
To convert Celsius to Fahrenheit: x 9 ÷ 5 + 32		

more convenient. The minibus leaves as soon as it is full, and the driver will drop you off anywhere along the route.

Ferries: For a country with so much coastline, Turkey has surprisingly few regular ferry services. But all of these are good. The best is the Istanbul ferry, which runs along the Black Sea coast as far as Trabzon. This service operates during the summer only (mid-April to mid-October). Seasonal ferries also run from Istanbul to the Marmara Islands in the Sea of Marmara. There is a regular link between Istanbul and the Princes' Islands, and between Istanbul and Izmir all year round.

Trains: This is the forgotten part of Turkey's transport system. And rightly so. Rail links cover a surprisingly wide network, linking all of the major cities, and several of the lesser ones. However, the system is rather slow and erratic. Train prices are about the same as bus fares.

Business Hours

Office hours are 09:00–18:00, Monday–Friday. Shops are usually open from 09:00–19:00, though some stay open much later in the resorts. Museums are usually open 09:30–16:30 Tuesday–Sunday. The same hours generally apply for palaces, except that they tend to be closed on Thursdays. Open-air sites are mostly open from 09:00–sunset. Some may be closed out of season. Always check up before setting out.

USEFUL PHRASES

Günaydın • Good day
Allaha ısmarladık • Goodbye
Kaç lira? •
How much does it cost?
Şerefinize! • Cheers!
İngilizce bilen bir kimse nerede? • Where is someone
who understands English?
Tuvalet nerede? •
Where is the toilet?
Bir otel nerede? •
Where is a hotel?
Havaalanı nerede? •
Where is the airport?
Kaç saat? •
How long will it take?
Benzin nerede? •
Where can I find petrol?

Time Difference

All of Turkey falls into one time zone, which is two hours ahead of Greenwich Mean (or Universal Standard) Time (GMT).

Communications

Post offices are open weekdays 09:00–17:00. Convenient metered **phone booths** (card- or coin-operated) are usually found in the post offices of large towns and resorts. For an international line dial 99. Turkish telephone numbers are at present undergoing transformation, which means that although the telephone numbers given in this guide are the most up-to-date, they may well change. Although Turkey has officially entered the age of the **fax**, unfortunately most of its inhabitants have not, and you would be unwise to rely on communication by this medium.

Electricity

220 volts, 50 AC. Plugs are two-pronged, but there are two different sizes, and correspondingly two different sizes of socket. These are in no way compatible (even if you push very hard). The smaller size is the same as that used by most of Europe.

Weights And Measures

Turkey uses the metric system.

Health Precautions

There are few serious health hazards in Turkey, although many visitors experience minor attacks of **diarrhoea** – usually owing to the change of climate and diet. Bring your favourite tablets with you. If you suffer from any more serious complaint, visit a *klinik* or *hastane* (**hospital**), indicated by a blue sign with a white 'H' in both instances. The very basic public service is free, the infinitely superior private service will cost you (or your insurance company). The reception desk at a private hospital will be able to provide you with a list of local private doctors. Be sure to ask for one who speaks your language. Mosquitoes can be bad in some places. In the countryside, the dogs are liable to have **rabies**. Encounters with snakes and scorpions are rare, and, as with most animals, they rarely bite unless they feel threatened. Take your usual protection against **sunburn**. Tap **water** is not universally safe to drink. Enquire first and, if in doubt, stock up on bottled water.

In the central city areas and main resorts you will find newsstands selling most of the international papers. These tend to arrive one day late. Also on sale, here and in bookshops, are a few English paperbacks. Foreign films are usually, but not always, dubbed in Turkish. Satellite TV is widely available with an attractive range of English-language programmes.

Personal Safety

Despite the horror stories of old, Turkey has a good, if not exceptional record for personal safety. Male chauvinism is still very much alive and pinching and, whether they want it or not, single women will attract attention. In the resort areas, where the locals are becoming increasingly used to Western habits, this may not be so bad. Outside these areas, especially out in the country, a woman is inviting trouble if she wanders off the beaten track on her own, or even with a female companion. The resorts tend to have their disco alleys, where tourist drunks are the main hazard. The red light districts in big cities, such as Istanbul, should be entered in male-only groups. Mugging is much less frequent than in Western countries, but it's worth taking the usual precautions. Walking around alone at night, with a lot of money in your pocket, is asking for trouble.

Emergencies

In the case of emergencies or accidents, it is advisable to call the **police**, tel: 155. They are often unexpectedly partial to the visitor's point of view. Always report any theft to the local police (or Tourist Police, who can be very helpful). Make sure you obtain an official piece of paper from them if you intend to claim from your insurance back home. The **fire brigade** may be telephoned on 110, and the **ambulance** on 112.

Best Buys

Leatherwear such as shoes, belts and hats are good and inexpensive. Jackets and coats are also amazingly cheap, but you can't rely on them being cut too well, so always try them on in front of a mirror first. Jewellery shops abound: the Turks prefer to keep their money in something a little more solid than currency. With a few notable exceptions, jewellery designs are distinctly ordinary. Shirts and jeans are cheap and good; local waistcoats are very good. Turkish carpets and kilims are world renowned, and tend to be priced accordingly. Inexpensive kilims are well worth the price. The best cheap gift are spices. These often come in an unfolding sachet of plastic packets which can be hung in the kitchen. The local tiles are exceptional, though their designs are invariably traditional. Other local ceramics tend to be unexceptional, and the brass is best worn by horses.

One	• *Bir*
Two	• *İki*
Three	• *Üç*
Four	• *Dört*
Five	• *Beş*
Six	• *Altı*
Seven	• *Yedi*
Eight	• *Sekiz*
Nine	• *Dokuz*
10	• *On*
11	• *On bir*
12	• *On iki*
20	• *Yirmi*
30	• *Otuz*
40	• *Kırk*
50	• *Elli*
60	• *Altmış*
70	• *Yetmiş*
80	• *Seksen*
90	• *Doksan*
100	• *Yüz*
110	• *Yüz on*
200	• *İki yüz*
300	• *Üç yüz*
1000	• *Bin*
2000	• *İki Bin*
1,000,000	• *Bir milyon*

GOOD READING

- Kemal, Yaşar (1990) *Mehmet My Hawk*. Collins.
- Stark, Freya (1991) *Alexander's Path*. Arrow.
- Norwich, John Julius (1995) *Byzantium, the Decline and Fall*. Viking.
- Lord Kinross (1990) *Atatürk, the Rebirth of a Nation*. Weidenfeld.
- Loti, Pierre (1989) *Aziyade*. KPI Paperbacks.
- Macaulay, Rose (1990) *The Towers of Trebizond*. Flamingo.
- Hikmet, Nazim (1990) *A Sad State of Freedom*. Greville Press.
- Bean, George E (1989) *Aegean Turkey*. Benn.